HORSES
OF
TODAY

Books by MARGARET CABELL SELF

Technical
TEACHING THE YOUNG TO RIDE
HORSES, THEIR SELECTION, CARE AND HANDLING
FUN ON HORSEBACK
HORSEMASTERSHIP
RIDING SIMPLIFIED
THE AMERICAN HORSE SHOW
JUMPING SIMPLIFIED
RIDING WITH MARILES
THE HORSEMAN'S ENCYCLOPEDIA
THE COMPLETE BOOK OF HORSES AND PONIES
HORSEBACK RIDING SIMPLIFIED
HORSES OF TODAY

Adult Fiction
COME AWAY
RED CLAY COUNTY
THOSE SMITH KIDS

Juvenile Fiction
CHITTER CHAT STORIES
PONIES ON PARADE
THE HAPPY YEAR (with Dennis Stock)

Miscellaneous
THE HORSEMAN'S COMPANION
A TREASURY OF HORSE STORIES
A WORLD OF HORSES
IRISH ADVENTURE

HORSES OF TODAY

Arabian, Thoroughbred
Saddle Horse, Standardbred
Western, Pony

by MARGARET CABELL SELF

DUELL, SLOAN AND PEARCE
NEW YORK

First Edition

Affiliate of
MEREDITH PRESS
Des Moines & New York

Library of Congress Catalogue Card Number: 64-18478

MANUFACTURED IN THE UNITED STATES OF AMERICA FOR MEREDITH PRESS

CONTENTS

HORSES
OF
TODAY

The Strange Survival of the Horse

The horse is one of the world's oldest surviving mammals. He antedates man and the other primates by millions of years. Since his domestication, somewhat over five thousand years ago, he has been prominent in four fields: in transportation, hence also colonization; in war; agriculture, both on the range and on the farm; and sport. To the many uses for which the horse was found suitable we owe the existence of the modern breeds and types.

With the advent of motorized vehicles the horse's major role, a means of transportation both for short and long distances, was taken away. Early in the twentieth century it was predicted that with his disappearance off the roads and highways he would soon become a rarity and we would find him only in the zoos. And the zoo in Central Park does have a pony among its other farm animals.

With the substitution of mechanized cavalry (armored tanks and cannons transported by motor vehicles instead of being pulled by teams of horses), his second most important profession was taken from him.

To those horse lovers who deplored the carnage of the battlefield this latter move was all to the good. Unfortunately, though, it had a side effect. Not only in the United States, but in most of the other countries using a mounted cavalry, there were hundreds of thousands of farmers who, living in a neighborhood where there was an available purebred stallion, kept two or three broodmares. Some of the mares were purebred but many were not. These breeders knew that if their colts did not show enough promise to bring good prices as racehorses, hunters, jumpers, or show animals, they would always find a ready market for them as military animals. Now this market had disappeared. The breeder could still sell his purebred colts, but this necessitated high-class mares. In certain areas, where hunting was a favorite sport, there was a market for the halfbred that had the necessary attributes and conformation, but what about the run-of-the-mill colts that were good substantial animals but were not outstanding? With the Remount program of purebred stallions placed throughout the country discontinued, the number of colts produced annually by small breeders was materially reduced in a very few years.

In many parts of the country, especially along the Eastern Seaboard where it was popular, the sport of fox hunting was being squeezed out by the spurt in building which followed the First World War and returned again after the depression of the thirties. It looked as though the horse was destined for extinction, even in the field of sport, except on the race course and in the show ring. During the 1920's and 1930's, flat racing, steeplechasing, and harness racing all increased in popularity owing largely to organizations such as the Jockey Club and the National Trotting Association, whose rules governed the tracks, to the enormous purses now offered, and to the advent of the pari-mutuel machines. But only syndicates or millionaires could afford to breed, train, and race thoroughbreds. Was the horse to be relegated to the role of a luxury animal known personally only to a very few?

There remained, in the realm of sport, the horse show. In the 1920's there were, as there are today, two classes of horse shows: Recognized shows, sponsored by the American Horse Shows Association, and unrecognized shows.

To compete successfully in a Recognized show, one had to have money enough to buy a high-class animal and to pay a professional trainer for conditioning it. The unrecognized shows were mainly neighborhood affairs at which the prizes were donated trophies. A class of more than ten entries was unusual, children younger than fourteen years of age were a rarity, and the emphasis was on pleasure hacks and hunters generally ridden by adults.

The United States was then way behind Europe in the development of knowledgeable experts in the age-old art of equitation. The term dressage was unknown. The only type of course used to test Open Jumpers consisted of two jumps with wings placed on the two long walls of an oval or rectangular ring. The competitor entered, went twice around without changing direction, and left. This type of course was also used in advanced horsemanship classes over jumps.

In those days, before the end of the mounted cavalry, only the military could compete in the equestrian events of the Olympic Games. This meant that the International Show teams, through which riders and horses were given the experience needed for competition in the Olympics, were always composed of military riders. For the civilian rider there was little opportunity for correct instruction in advanced equitation, though every so often a European-trained instructor became available.

Then, with the discontinuance of the mounted cavalry, civilian riders became eligible to ride on the International Jumping teams. At the same time a curious thing occurred. Almost simultaneously and practically throughout the country, children of all ages suddenly discovered the romance and fascination of the horse.

It is a well-known fact that when a person finds himself on top of a horse, looking down at those on foot, something happens to him psychologically. His ego receives a tremendous boost; he becomes an important person. In the horse-and-buggy days, when almost every rural householder necessarily kept a horse of sorts, the very plentitude of horses and riders—good or bad—took away much of the importance of the horse as a psychological booster of the ego. This was all changed with the advent of the automobile and the consequent disappearance of the horse as a necessary servant.

In the early 1930's and somewhat later, first the radio and then television introduced the "horse opera." To the young all over the United States this sudden reappearance of the horse as a romantic ideal symbolizing an exciting world of adventure was irresistible. Even today, with competing interest in the space ship, the horse opera holds its own.

The Second World War with its restrictions on gasoline gave a further incentive. Many a family, thinking that a gentle animal hitched to a suitable vehicle would offset the scarcity of gasoline coupons, yielded to the pleas of their horse-crazy offspring and bought what they considered a good, safe animal.

And now the problems began. When Grandfather was a little boy, his father, whose education included care of horses, knew what to do when Dobbin got cast in the stall, tangled himself up in a fence, or showed symptoms of colic. Except in the Far West, however, Father did not have this training. He or Mother may have done a little riding in the park or in a local riding school, but neither had the faintest idea what they were going in for when they built a stall in the unused part of the garage.

Most of the members of this newly-formed band of horse owners gave up after a few months and sold their horses or ponies. But their children were still spellbound. They wanted to continue riding. And their friends, also fascinated, joined them in applying for instruction at riding schools and hunt clubs. Those who had envisioned themselves galloping across country *à la* cowboy in a lesson or two were quickly disillusioned. They found that learning to become a good or even a passable rider was a long, tedious, often uncomfortable, and sometimes rather terrifying process. The boys especially, who had less patience than the girls and to whom the schools offered diversion in the form of organized sports, often lost interest. But for the girls riding was an ideal sport. They were quite contented to trot around and around while they were learning to "talk horse language." The psychological boost was enormous, not only finding themselves atop a horse but also discovering that, with patience, they could learn to control an animal far larger and stronger than themselves. Furthermore, here was a sport in which, as a sex, they were not handicapped in competition. Indeed they often showed greater sensitivity which made them excel over the boys, especially in the show ring.

Of course, many of the so-called riding stables that offered "instruction" were, and still are, completely inadequate. Their owners knew nothing about equitation and were interested only in getting the dollar or two per hour, which was the charge for going out under the guidance of a stable boy on an underfed spiritless animal.

But many good riding schools sprang up. Private schools and camps often had excellent riding programs, and many hunt clubs, no longer able to maintain a pack without open country, found themselves suddenly reactivated by this interest in learning to ride.

Now the whole picture began to change. Breeders and trainers, realizing the demand for suitable children's mounts, commenced raising well-bred animals, both horses and ponies, and training them especially for this market. Pony clubs sprang up in every direction. 4-H clubs, hitherto devoted solely to the raising of farm animals, suddenly became interested in learning how to care for horses and how to ride. Breeding associations often assisted by donating high-class animals for this purpose.

Above all, the interest in showing increased, both in the registered and in the unregistered shows. Also, now that civilian riders might be selected for international competition, the interest in classes for Open Jumpers took a spurt. As far back as 1945, sixty or seventy entries in an "open" class were not unknown. In the middle 1950's the "pet" or "hunter type" pony came into its own. Previously a class of twelve ponies of different heights, ranging from the tiny ten-hand Shetland to the larger pony of fourteen hands two inches, had been a rarity. In 1960, in many communities, pony classes all had to be divided three ways according to height, and classes of from thirty-five to fifty ponies in each division were not uncommon. This astounding increase of entries was due to the number of children under twelve who had become good riders and also to the enormous number of well-bred ponies that had now become available.

Currently, it is not only in pony classes that the young rider is rapidly supplanting the adult. Professional riders still predominate in the Open Jumper classes, in American Saddle and in Shetland Pony (Harness Type) as well as Fine Harness and Hackney classes. These classes, however, are fairly well confined to the larger shows. In the local shows, both Recognized and unrecognized, at least two-thirds of the prizes offered are for equitation on the flat or over jumps, for dressage, for children's jumpers, and for hunters or hacks. Of course, in the Western classes the halter, breed, and performance classes predominate, and here, although there are many riders in their teens, there are also plenty of adults.

It is not only the pony that has become popular with breeders. There is a tremendous upsurge in the number of horses registered in practically every stud record—Morgans, Arabians, Palominos, Quarterhorses, American Saddle Horses, Standardbreds, Thoroughbreds, Half-breds. The breeding associations are exceedingly active and constantly thinking of new ways to promote their breeds. One example of this is the interest in racing other than Thoroughbred racing. There is Quarterhorse racing under the auspices of the American Quarterhorse Association, and the very recently formed Pinto Horse Association has begun to promote interest in races limited to spotted horses.

The Arabian is another breed of horse that has become increasingly popular, almost solely through the stimulus of Horse Show competition. Although the first Arabians were imported along with the first Thoroughbreds, the breed never became very popular, and a purebred Arabian was a rarity up until about fifteen years ago. Today there are Arabian horse associations in practically every state and two national associations. Particularly in the West, classes limited to Arabians are becoming more and more popular. There are also a number of all Arabian shows being held in various parts of the country.

It is difficult to see where all this is leading. The very popularity of the Horse Show is beginning to be a major problem. Big shows, in spite of the most careful organization, often run three or four hours late, due to the unpredictable number of entries. Where will it all end? Will this tremendous mushrooming of the numbers of horses brought to the shows lead to the gradual extinction of the shows? Or will the American Horse Show Association (AHSA), the Cutting Horse Association, and others find a way to conduct these tests without having groups of youngsters under thirteen years of age kept waiting until twelve midnight to enter an Equitation class scheduled to start at seven in the evening?

The AHSA realizes the danger and is doing its best by increasing the qualifications required in certain classes. To compete for the Maclay Cup at Madison Square Garden, for example, a young rider must first have won the class in three other Recognized shows. Before the class is held, there is an elimination class, and the contestants, last year numbering about seventy, are cut down to a number to which the judges can give fair consideration in the hour allotted on the program. As time goes on, no doubt such conditions will have to be imposed upon practically all classes in the larger shows. Another solution might be to have "specialty shows." But here we run into the problem of the necessity for variety to keep the audience interested.

The horse show picture is quite different abroad and in Central and South America. In many of these countries classes are limited to competition in open jumping, cross country jumping, dressage tests and combined training tests. These competitions are very popular and draw huge crowds. No doubt the number of such shows will increase in the United States, and there is already a great interest in the combined training shows, still very new here. Yet such shows cannot solve the big problem of how to handle the tremendous number of entries to be found in all other classes.

Contrary to predictions, the horse has survived and the equine population in the United States is still strongly on the upswing. The purpose of this book is to discuss each breed popular today, not only generally and historically, but on a more personal basis as well. Horses are not machines. One cannot order them by vintage, size, or number. Those who breed, raise, and train horses professionally are experts, but usually experts on one particular breed or type. The Thoroughbred trainer, preparing his two-year-olds for the track, has nothing in common with the professional trainer of a five-gaited American Saddle Horse except that, in each case, the horses are a means of livelihood. They are not necessarily personalities to him in the way that the favorite mount is a personality to the amateur.

It has been my good fortune to know, work with, and study individuals of all of the popular modern breeds. I have looked on them as friends and as servants, expecting them to carry out their work; but I have learned, too, that their individual physical and temperamental characteristics must be taken into consideration in planning this work. I have come to the conclusion that a colt is never born vicious or mean, though many become untrustworthy from ignorant or brutal handling. The brain of the horse may be small, but he uses what he has, and the longer I work these animals, the more I realize their capacities. In this book I have given short "profiles" of some of my favorite horses. I dedicate it to them and also to the amateur who, though he will find his life tremendously enriched through his close association with horses, must be prepared to pay the penalty when the time comes for his friend and companion to leave for the green pastures of *ultima Thule.*

Budd

Misr, *an Arabian saddle horse*

CHAPTER 1

The Arabian Division

The Arabian Horse

It is fitting that any book dealing with different breeds of horses should begin with a discussion of the Arabian, for his blood is to be found in all "light" horses of today. His is the oldest and purest breed, as Arabs of the desert have been interested in keeping it pure for nearly five thousand years. So high are the breeders' ideals in this line that no mare bred to an "impure" stallion is ever considered able to produce an *asil* (pure) foal in the future, even though the future breedings might be to a purebred stallion. For this reason, from the Arab's standpoint, there are very few completely pure Arabian horses in Arabia today and none have ever been sold. However, breeders of other lands are not particular, and any Arabian horse descended from pure Arabian or desert stock is considered pure. In Poland, for example, no mention is made of the exact name of either sire or dam in the pedigree, even though the dealer may supply these with authenticated papers. It is considered enough to say *Or. Ar.* meaning "Original Arab." For many years it was impossible to buy Arabian mares for importation. The bloodlines have always been carried back through the mares in Arabia rather than through the stallions. The Arab valued his mare much more highly than he did his stallions, not only for this reason but also because she was more suitable for his use as a "war" animal. Warfare in the desert meant unexpected raids either on herds or on tribes living in their portable tents. Therefore, the horseman when reconnoitering or guarding his herd of camels or horses, rode a mare rather than a stallion, for the latter was more apt to trumpet at the approach of another horse. Furthermore, the mare was considered a member of the household; she slept beside her master in his tent and was trained as a watchdog and not considered just a beast of burden. Under such circumstances she was gentler than the stallion.

HISTORY AND ORIGIN

No one knows exactly when horses first came to Arabia nor where they came from, but it is believed that they originated in India. According to folklore God gave Arabia and the Arabic language to Ishmael, son of Abraham. Ishmael, who became a hunter, built an Ark of the Desert in honor of his Creator. God then asked the Angel Gabriel to lend one of the horses of heaven to Ishmael in recognition of his fealty. When Gabriel descended to the desert where Ishmael lay sleeping, "a wind came up from the west scattering dust with a blast from its nostrils and screaming with ferocity." Gabriel grasped the wind in his hands, and it emerged in the form of a mare. When Ishmael awoke, he took her for an antelope (from which we deduce that she was fawn colored or brownish) and was about to shoot her with his bow and arrow when Gabriel interfered and explained to him that she was not to be hunted but would be a "mother of bounty and blessings, a destroyer of enemies and a vessel of joy." Furthermore, he prophesied that the mare would produce a black foal and that they should be the progenitors of a new race of creatures.

The tribe was on the move when the foal was born, and it was put in a camel sack. At the end of the day, when it was taken out of the sack, the foal was a cripple, with an injured spine. Ishmael again was about to destroy it and again was restrained by the Angel Gabriel. As had been prophesied, the mare and her son became the founders of the whole race of Arabian horses, unknown before in the desert. Ishmael himself became known as Faris (rider of the *fara*, or mare).

There are five recognized strains of the Arabian horse. These are the Kuhaylan, Saqlawi, 'Ubanyan, Hamdani, and Hadban. They are named for the original five mares chosen as foundation mares. The legend concerning their selection runs as follows:

Burr Betts

In a western setting, the Arabian Ankthor *makes a perfect trail horse.*

Arabian racing at Laurel, Maryland

Five generations after the presentation of the first mare to Ishmael, Salaman (sometimes confused with Soloman and also known as Faris, or "horseman") had been traveling for many days over the desert. His horses and mares were frantic with thirst, when finally they came to the brink of a river. Just as they were about to plunge into it to quench their thirst, the trumpet sounded the call to arms. Five of the mares left the river without drinking to respond to its summons. It was these five which were selected by Faris to found the five strains of purebred Arabian horses. Naturally each strain had many offshoots, but in every case the family retained a suffix denoting the original strain from which it was derived.

DEVELOPMENT

In discussing the type of horse into which the Arabian developed and which has characterized him for the last two or three thousand years, one must take into consideration his environment and the use for which he was bred. In breeding, the Arab took the pedigree as the deciding factor rather than the actual appearance of a given mare or stallion. Each of the five strains was noted in particular for one special trait, such as strength, stamina, speed, intelligence, etc., or for a combination of these. It was the ancestry displaying the traits he wished either to improve or introduce in the foal which decided the Arab breeder's choice of stallion or mare. Naturally he

International Arabian Horse Association

was interested in producing the ideal horse not only from the point of view of beauty but principally from the point of view of usefulness. What, then, did he consider desirable, and how did this selective breeding affect the resulting animal both physically and temperamentally?

The Arab wanted an intelligent animal, one that would always be on the alert to warn him of the approach of an enemy. In considering intelligence he reasoned that since the brain is situated behind the forehead, a bulging forehead was important, as it would give more room for gray matter. This bulge, known as the *jibbah,* is emphasized by a hollowness where the nasal bones are attached to the skull. It is one of the outstanding characteristics of the profile of an Arabian's head.

Since hearing and eyesight are both extremely important in an animal considered a watchdog, the Arab bred for small, alert, well-pricked ears and very large, wide-set, bulging eyes. Every horseman knows that the alert animal pricks his ears the instant he hears anything to arouse his curiosity. There is a great difference in the individual animals in this respect. Some bad-tempered beasts carry their ears pinned back most of the time, being more interested in warning their companions or showing dislike of what the rider is communicating than in paying attention to what goes on around them. Others are naturally lazy and slow and carry their ears relaxed. Not so the Arabian horse; he constantly pricks up his ears and they are so curved and pointed that often the tips nearly meet. The horse's eyes, being set on the side of the head, have a much wider range of vision than human eyes. This is augmented by the fact that these horses' eyes bulge out and are not set deep in the skull for protection. Naturally the larger and more bulging the eye, the wider range of vision.

Speed and the ability to get away to a quick start were high in the attributes desired by the Arab breeder. This necessitated a thin, sensitive skin and a rapid gait. The trot is not a natural gait of the Arabian horse. In his native desert he walks, ambles, and gallops. His walk is active and long and characterized by a pronounced swinging of the head from side to side. The latter characteristic was encouraged by the rider, as it enlarged the periphery of the horse's vision and so made it easier for him to notice anything unusual that might occur on the distant horizon. The gallop was characterized by both its speed and its quick start.

Although the trot was not a gait natural to the desert horse, the Arabian did develop a trot, and its most outstanding characteristic is its "floating" action. In classical dressage this is a major and most important type of movement, from which is developed the "passage." It is the opposite of the pounding, high-kneed action of the Hackney and Saddle Horse. The horse, after lifting the feet, throws them forward, and there is a perceptible hesitation as the weight passes from one diagonal to the other. It is a movement frequently seen in horses running loose in pasture. When something excites their curiosity, they will often approach in this slow, measured, beautifully cadenced trot.

Not only must the horse of the desert be able to get away to a quick start and to develop speed, but he must be able to keep it up for miles in order to outrun or to overtake the enemy. Three major factors influence the horse's wind. He must have wide, flaring nostrils in order to suck in plenty of air. He must have a big "throttle" and windpipe, and he must have a deep, broad chest and barrel to provide plenty of room for his lungs. So the Arab breeder bred for these characteristics. He was especially interested in the throttle, that point under the neck where the latter joins the head. His ideal was that the curve of the crest on top of the neck be repeated in a wide curve at the throttle. Only thus could there be a free passage of air to the lungs. This type of throttle is the exact opposite of what is known as a "hammer-headed" type of animal.

Forage is scarce in desert countries. Smaller horses need less food than larger ones, but if they are to carry the weight of a full-grown man, they

Budd

Indy Mac *jumps at the Devon Show.*

An Arabian horse, Al Marah Nizar, *works at round-up on the range.*

must have strong backs. The average Arabian stallion is between fourteen-two and fifteen hands in height, mares are often somewhat smaller. The Arabian horse has one fewer dorsal vertebrae than does the horse of other breeds. The tail is high set and the croup, from point of croup to dock, is more level than that of the Thoroughbred or Standardbred. These all make up a sturdy animal. The tail is held away from the buttocks, probably because Arabia is a hot country and the Arabian horse does not need to clutch his tail in to his buttocks for warmth as does the Icelandic pony. Since the Arabian sun is strong, one of the characteristics of the Arabian is a dark skin, this being less liable to sunburn than a light skin. The Arabian has strength and a remarkable hardiness, for in his natural habitat he can live

International Arabian Horse Association

on very little. It is said that he can go longer without food and water and still maintain his strength than any other breed.

As for his temperamental characteristics, the Arabian is surprisingly intelligent, since for generations he has been treated like a member of the family. Normally he trusts man rather than fears him. He learns very quickly and is willing to learn. He is readily teachable when it comes to tricks, also, loving to "pose" on a pedestal, to bow, etc., and seeming to appreciate applause. In reactions he is extraordinarily quick. The Arabian reacts to "the wind of the rider's spur," as the expression goes. For this reason, gentle as he is, he is not an ideal mount for a beginner.

USES

To what use have these horses been put after leaving the desert countries?

The Arabian's first and most important characteristic is his prepotency, his ability to pass his traits on to his descendents. For this reason he has been used all over the world to improve other breeds of horse. There is not a single "light" horse today in this country whose ancestry does not run back to Arabian stock. Standardbred, Saddlebred, and Morgan Hackney are all offshoots either of the Arabian directly or of the Thoroughbred. As everyone knows, all English Thoroughbreds are descendents of the European mare and either the Darley Arabian, the Godolphin Barb, or the Byerly Turk, a stallion imported into England from the desert in the middle eighteenth century.

In the New World there were no horses until the coming of Cortes and the conquistadores who followed him. They brought with them horses from Spain. These, in turn, were the descendants of the horses which the Moors brought with them when they conquered Spain and ruled it for over five hundred years. So the wild mustang from whom is descended the Western stock horse also has Arabian ancestry.

TYPES

Today's Arabian horses vary greatly in type, because they are used for widely different purposes. Breeders specialize in developing animals suitable for specific purposes; therefore, by selective breeding, they come up with Arabians which in some cases differ greatly from the original desert animal. There are some breeders, for example, who would turn the Arab into a small Saddle Horse, for Saddle Horse riders are beginning to appear in shows riding Arabians in classes specifically held for these horses. Many true lovers of the breed think this is a mistake. By breeders' letting the feet grow too long and putting on weighted shoes such horses lose their natural "floating" gait for which they are noted and gain nothing to take its place. Nevertheless, the Arabian horse is making himself useful.

To begin with, he is an outstanding pleasure and "trail" horse. He has been outstanding in distance rides such as the Vermont one hundred-mile Trail Ride, held every year in that state to test the stamina and endurance

Jumping is demonstrated by the Arabian, Manolette.

of horses traveling over natural country. Since he is very smooth-gaited and gentle, he is an ideal pleasure horse; and as he is hardy, he does not lose condition as does the Thoroughbred, when not kept on a high grain diet.

There is a tremendous interest in Arabian racing both in this country and in Europe. In spite of his speed the Arabian cannot hope to compete against the Thoroughbred because of the former's shorter stride. But races for Arabians alone are becoming very popular. These races are often for two or two and a half miles so that the endurance and stamina are tested as well as the speed.

Tasamar, *an example of the Arabian stock horse*

AS A SHOW HORSE

As "parade horse" and also on the range as a "stock horse," the Arabian is very popular. However, it is in the horse shows that one finds the widest divergence of use. The following is a list of classes and divisions in which Arabians won or placed in a recent big show in the West:

Western Stock	Driving, Informal: juniors to drive
Cutting Horse	Driving, Formal
Equitation, Western	English Equitation
Parade	Three-Gaited Saddle
Pleasure Horse	Equitation, Side Saddle
Combination	Dressage

A Polish Arabian horse, Witez II, *displays his breed characteristics.*

Of course, there were also Arabian breed classes.

I have also seen pictures of Arabians that were hunted regularly. In my own stable I have had two Arabians of which I was very fond. One was a little mare lent to me one winter many years ago. Her name was Scherazade, and she was the first purebred Arabian I had ever known well. What a delight she was! This was a horse one could ride all day and never become tired or bored. Hitherto I had thought that all Arabians had "choppy" gaits, but Scherazade had the true floating gait of her race. She was as gentle as a kitten but quick as a flash of lightning.

Ten years ago I bought a young Arabian stallion. I broke and trained him myself, and he is still one of my favorite mounts. He is so gentle that we can put a child on him in a group of twenty horses and do games or close-order drill. He has been on our dressage quadrille team as well as on our formation jumping team. He understands English as well as an intelligent dog, and he does everything on vocal commands. I have taught him a few circus stunts simply because he loves to show off. When on his back, it is only necessary to think, and he will obey.

Polish-Arabian

Although this book is primarily about horses in the United States, the Polish-Arabian horses should be mentioned. For many years Poland has been intensely interested in the importation, breeding, and racing of desert-bred Arabian horses. Since World War II breeders in this country have become very interested in these Polish-Arabian and many have been imported.

The Morab

The Morab is a cross between the Morgan and the Arabian. Some specimens take after the desert horse, some after the Morgan. Although I have never had a Morab of my own and so cannot tell from personal experience, they seem to make excellent general-purpose and trail horses, especially for children. They are extremely hardy, not so sensitive as the purebred Arabian, and less opinionated than some of the Morgans.

The Anglo-Arab

The Anglo-Arab is a cross between the Thoroughbred and Arabian. Many people prefer this cross to either purebred, saying that the resulting animal is less hysterical and more intelligent than the Thoroughbred, bigger and with a better jump than the Arabian. I have seen many on the hunt field and they have always been outstanding animals. Here again the types differ, depending on which parent was the more prepotent. The International Arab Horse Association registers both these, the Morab and the Anglo-Arab, in their Arabian Half-bred registry.

Breeders of ponies also like to cross the Arabian with both Welsh and Shetlands. When these turn out well, they are very good indeed, especially for the skilled rider. However, I have seen a few results of this cross that tended to be weedy and to inherit the worst traits of both parents.

Clubs and Associations

Nearly every state has its own Arabian Horse Club. There are, in addition to these, three other associations. One, the International Arabian Horse Association, is located at 224 East Olive Avenue, Burbank, California. It publishes the *Arabian Horse Year Book* as well as a number of interesting brochures. One of these, *Arabs and What They Can Do*, gives rules for judging Arabian horses as well as discussing their various aptitudes. *The Arab Horse Journal*, under the sponsorship of the International Arabian Horse Association, is published by the Cruse Publishing Company. It appears eleven times a year and contains many interesting and instructive articles on the breed. One issue each year is devoted to the stallions standing throughout the country.

The Arabian Horse Club Registry of America, whose address is 120 South La Salle Street, Chicago 3, Illinois, has been in existence for more than fifty years. It keeps the registration records of the purebred Arabian horse, and altogether has registered more than twenty-three thousand of them. In 1962 there were twenty-five hundred new registrations, and the growing interest in this breed is shown in the average increase of 25 per cent of new registrations during the past few years.

The Arabian Horse Club is particularly interested in encouraging the breeding of the classical type of Arabian, rather than in trying to change him into something else.

The Arabian Horse Owners Foundation is a nonprofit organization whose purpose is to improve the management and understanding of the Arabian horse. It does this by means of short courses or seminars which horse lovers or owners may attend. Lectures and demonstrations given by qualified veterinarians or trainers include such subjects as shoeing, parasites, training (advanced), care of equipment, breeding program, foaling,"do's and don'ts," endurance rides, conformation and soundness, nutrition, etc. A diploma is issued at the end of the three-day course.

The address of the association changes with the president, who currently is Gina (Mrs. Clarence) Manion, 51187 Laurel Road, South Bend, Indiana.

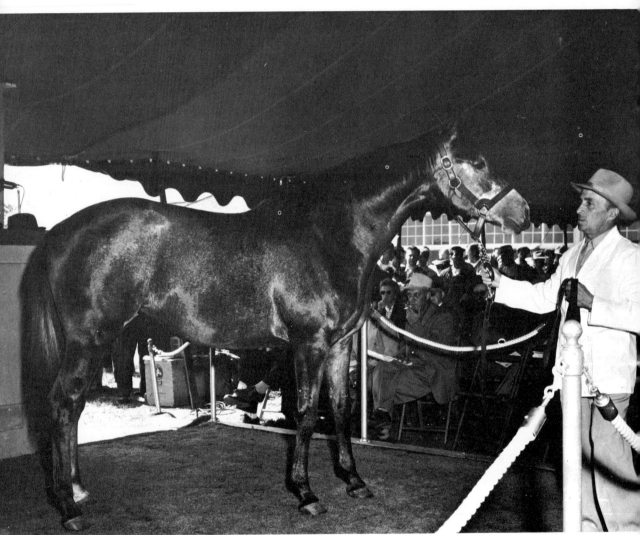

Almond Eyes, *a thoroughbred filly, is shown at an auction.*

CHAPTER 2

The Thoroughbred Division

The Thoroughbred

ORIGIN AND HISTORY

The Thoroughbred is the only horse of today whose original and present primary uses are the same. Racing is the oldest organized sport in which horses are used. The English Thoroughbred resulted from the crossing of the blood of desert stallions with English and European mares. This started in the twelfth century and can be traced back to the Crusaders. Many desert stallions and some mares of both Arab and Barb breeding were imported, though none were what the Arab considered *asil* (pure). Mating was more or less by trial and error. However, in the seventeenth century three desert stallions were imported whose names are destined to live forever in the equine halls of fame. The first of these was a horse known as the Byerly Turk. He is supposed to have been captured from the Turks in 1685 and to have been used as a cavalry mount in Ireland by Captain Byerly in 1689. The second, the Darley Arabian, was imported as a four-year old in 1704 by Thomas Darley. His actual pedigree and history are not entirely clear. It is thought that he may have been of Turkish or Syrian blood rather than Arabian.

The Godolphin Barb (sometimes called the Godolphin Arabian) is thought to have been discovered in Paris in 1728, pulling a water cart. From this plebeian fate he was rescued by a Mr. Coke, although no one knows how he got to Paris in the first place. Eventually he ended up in the stud of the Earl of Godolphin, where he was used for breeding for many years and from whom he received his distinguished name.

To understand why it is these three stallions whose names we know today and not those of the many others also used to develop the running horse, one must understand the expression "tail-male" line in relation to pedigrees. This simply means that the pedigree is traced from father to son. (In Arabia the pedigrees are the "tail-female" line, or mother to daughter.) All Thoroughbreds trace their lineage back through the generations from son to father to grandfather, etc., directly to one of these three stallions, and to no other. And since many of our other breeds, Standardbred, Saddlebred, etc., are derived from the Thoroughbred, these, too, can claim the blood of one of the three foundation sires.

Even more remarkable, each of the three original desert stallions had only one direct descendent, whose name appears in every pedigree of that line. Herod, foaled in 1758, was the great-great-grandson of Byerly Turk. The tail-male line of the Godolphin Barb leads through his grandson Matchem, foaled in 1748, while Eclipse, foaled in 1767, is the great-great-grandson of the Darley Arabian, and is the common ancestor of all horses whose bloodlines can be followed to the Darley Arabian.

It might be wise, at this time, to clear up the confusion so often found in the use of the word "thoroughbred" as an adjective, and the word Thoroughbred (often not capitalized) to mean a distinctive breed of horse as opposed to other breeds. The adjective "thoroughbred" is used to mean "purebred." Thus one hears the expression "thoroughbred collie." The noun Thoroughbred means a horse whose lineage both on the side of his sire and his dam can be traced straight back to one of the three foundation sires mentioned. A "registered Thoroughbred" is a Thoroughbred which has been registered with the Jockey Club and whose owner holds a pedigree or Registration Certificate describing the animal and showing its lineage.

The first edition of the *General* (English) *Stud Book* was published in 1793 by the Jockey Club of England, formed in Newmarket in 1750. The *Stud Book* featured a new breed of horse—the English Thoroughbred—developed primarily for racing. The name was logical, since the main purpose of the registration of animals in a stud book was to keep the bloodlines pure and prevent the introduction of any outside blood.

TYPE

Let us now discuss what type of animal this newly developed English Thoroughbred was. From his desert-bred ancestors he inherited speed, sensi-

The thoroughbred Tulyarta, *daughter of the famous Irish stallion* Tulyar, *wins at Aqueduct, New York.*

tivity, spirit, and intelligence. His native-bred maternal ancestors contributed, among other attributes, size and length of leg. The result was the fastest animal yet to appear on the tracks. Physically these early Thoroughbreds more nearly resembled their Arabian ancestors than do the Thoroughbreds of today. This is readily understandable, since they were closer to the original pure desert strains. In early paintings we notice that, generally speaking, their heads were apt to be finer and more Arabian in type and the whole animal often more lightly built than are many of our modern Thoroughbreds. However, Thoroughbreds usually have the same outstanding physical characteristics as their ancestors. These include a fine, lean, bony head, well set on; a good neck, neither long and stringy nor short and heavy, with a good crest; a sloping shoulder; deep chest (as seen from the side), with plenty of width (as seen from the front), but not too much. His ribs are well sprung and his barrel ribbed up. His croup is pear-shaped with a lower-set tail than that of

It's Decidedly *moves rhythmically along Churchill Downs.*

Wide World Photo

the Arab. The line from buttock point to stifle and buttock point to hip is long. Seen from the side, his cannon bones are short, wide, and flat. A plumb line dropped from the point of the buttock would pass at or behind the point of the hock. (In the Standardbred and Saddlers this line generally passes about through the middle of the hock.) His action is not high, nor does he carry his head abnormally high when moving.

The above description is considered ideal conformation for the Thoroughbred. Naturally, individual specimens vary. Temperamentally there is also a great variation. Some follow their desert ancestry and are always on the alert, always sensitive, and quick to react. Others seem sluggish and "doggy," until something happens either to startle them or to disturb them, when they explode like firecrackers.

Perhaps because for so many generations the Thoroughbred has been coddled and kept in stables, he is less hardy under natural conditions than

Decimal (*left*), *ridden by Dooley Adams, top steeplechase jockey.*

Wide World Photo

are many other breeds. His skin is so thin that flies drive him wild, and he will quickly lose condition when turned out in fly season. Nor does he prosper when asked to forage for himself. The tough little Stock horse will do his work day after day without grain, grooming, or stabling, living on grass or hay, and will stay in hard condition, but the Thoroughbred under such circumstances loses his spirit and his flesh until he looks and acts like a wraith of his former self.

It is also claimed, and with justice, that the Thoroughbred is more subject to hysteria and has less "horse-sense" than other horses. To my mind, however, this ties in with his tremendous "heart"—his unwillingness to give in—which has made him outstanding as a racer. There are records of horses that have continued to run even after breaking a leg, crossing the finish line and then collapsing. There was another well-known race horse that was unaccountably unpredictable; some days he would lead the field, other days he could hardly finish. He died suddenly after a race and an autopsy showed that he had only one healthy lung. Yet his "heart" had carried him through. Small wonder, then, that the Thoroughbred who finds himself cast and unable to rise struggles until he dies rather than give in.

Uses

Because of these temperamental and physical characteristics, the Thoroughbred is rarely a suitable animal for the less experienced rider or for the horseman who wants a "trail horse," one on which he can amble through the woods and fields without having to pay too much attention to his mount. The horseman mounted on a Thoroughbred must always be on the alert. He must learn to be a part of his horse so that the two react and move as one. And to such a horseman no other breed can compare with the Thoroughbred. No other type of mount can offer the satisfaction and the interest. The Thoroughbred not only has the speed and courage necessary for racing, but his great heart and his conformation make him suitable for jumping and hunting, and his sensitivity and willingness make him suitable for dressage.

How The Thoroughbred Developed In The New World

The Thoroughbred has had a long history in the United States. Cortes and other Spanish conquistadores introduced the horse into the New World.

The descendants of these horses became the Mustangs and the range horses of South America. Introduced to the Eastern Seaboard by the Colonials, some Thoroughbreds were imported for breeding purposes or for racing, and some were imported as cavalry mounts. Before 1893, racing had been under the rules of a Board of Control. In December of that year a meeting of owners and trainers was held, and the American Jockey Club was formed, based on the organization and methods of the Jockey Club of England. Its purpose was to encourage the development of the Thoroughbred horse through the establishment of racing on a footing which would promote that sport in such a manner that the public would enjoy and have confidence in it and, by providing a ready market, to encourage the breeders.

Today the Jockey Club, through its publication, *Rules of Racing*, governs the racing on all Recognized tracks. It has charge of all registrations of Thoroughbreds, the rules of the latter being laid out in a booklet called *The American Stud Book*. The *American Racing Manual*, compiled and published annually by the Daily Racing Form and copyrighted by Triangle Publications, gives complete statistics on everything concerning flat racing, including all horses, trainers, jockeys, owners, lists of tracks, records of all races, leading sires and broodmares of the year. Every bit of data pertaining to racing and all records of a given year are to be found between its covers.

Without racing, its large purses, and the innate love of competition which induces owners to spend millions in producing a fine horse, there would be few Thoroughbreds. But not all Thoroughbreds are destined to race. Many mares of pure ancestry are taken to the stud with no idea of training their foal for racing or selling him at the yearling sales. Mares of blood other than Thoroughbred are often mated with Thoroughbred stallions, the desire being to use the Thoroughbred blood to produce an animal which will make a good Hack or Hunter. This practice goes back over the centuries, so it is obvious that the Thoroughbred's second most important mission in life has not changed—to improve and develop types of horses other than purebreds. The Standardbred, as we shall see later, was first developed for private use; individual owners vied with each other in informal "brushes" on the streets of Harlem and at the country fairs. The Saddler came into being because the Southern gentleman-planter wanted a stylish, comfortable mount. The Morgan was a utility horse. But the Thoroughbred is still bred today for the same purposes as he was bred and used in the past.

Easy Going and Meadow Whisk

I have had a number of Thoroughbreds, but two of them stand out immediately. The first was a long, rangy, sixteen-hand Thoroughbred. I cannot recall his registered name, but we called him Easy Going. He had been bred in Virginia, found not fast enough for racing, and had been sent to New England to be turned into a Hunter. At one of the hunting stables there he met with his first major misfortune. Somehow he got a dose of lime in one eye when the stable was being whitewashed, and it blinded him. He had never been very satisfactory as a Hunter anyway, preferring to bounce his riders off rather than to bounce himself quietly over the jumps. When he became blinded, he was quickly traded off. I picked him up complete with papers for about a hundred dollars.

Apparently his accident had sobered him. Also, when I bought him, he was in very poor condition, and this, too, may have had something to do with his change in temperament. At any rate, he was so quiet and gentle that we called him Easy Going.

He proved still to be a bad-luck horse, for he was continually getting hurt. He had accidents that would have finished off a less courageous horse, most of which were probably due to his faulty eyesight. Furthermore, he seemed to develop nearly every bump, blemish, and enlargement known. Surprisingly enough, none of these affected his jumping, and his manners remained impeccable. He lived to be over twenty, and as a children's Open Jumper he was almost unbeatable.

The second Thoroughbred who will always live in my heart was a brave little stallion. Meadow Whisk was by Broom Whisk out of a mare that was only two generations removed from Man o' War. He was a small horse, only fourteen-two, and just what I was looking for to cross with pony mares and others for developing suitable small horses or large ponies. He was a color I have never seen before or since, though I once saw a photograph of an Arabian of that color. He might be described as a blood bay with undertones of blue, and in the sun his coat shone like purest copper.

When I bought "Whiskey," my younger daughter, Gincy, was twelve, and I turned him over to her for training. He was fairly well halter-broken, but that was all, and he had been raised by a farmer who had not bothered to groom him, so this, too, was a new experience. But he was one of the gentlest, most willing, and intelligent horses I have known. He soon lost his fear of the

Life magazine

Meadow Whisk *performs over a "mental hazard" course.*

grooming tools. In one easy lesson he learned what a longe was for. It was at the end of September that he was first introduced to the saddle, and at Thanksgiving time, that same year, my daughter rode him in a musical show carrying a lance.

In the spring of the following year she started his jumping, and then, for the first time, we really found out what we had bought. Whiskey jumped like a deer over anything he faced. One week before our annual Spring Circus, Gincy decided to train him for what we call a "mental hazard" exhibition. In this the jumps are all composed of the things that usually frighten the average horse: a clothesline complete with clothes blowing in the wind; an ironing board set up in an open space with no wings; a row of pails with loose stones in them hung on a rail which is swung as the horse approaches, causing the stones to rattle; a bicycle turned upside down, its spinning wheels strung with bright streamers of crepe paper; a spray of water from a hose; and a hoop wrapped with burlap which has been soaked in kerosene and then set on fire. These were a few of the obstacles we used, and Gincy announced that she thought a week was plenty of time to teach little Whiskey not to fear them. A week! It turned out that he didn't need any schooling. All she did was set up each obstacle and then jump it. He showed no fear at all! Only Sky Rocket, about whom I will talk later, ever showed such aptitude.

It was only shortly after this show, when we had had Whiskey for less than a year, that we learned his days were numbered, for he developed periodic ophthalmia. Less than a year and a half later he was completely blind in one eye and the other began to go. At the end of another two years he was stone blind. However, we kept him on for a while for breeding, though our facilities prevented us from having more than two foals a year. We got two very fine colts from a Half-bred range mare named Bonny, as well as Mooney, whose mother was a Hackney pony.

Through it all Whiskey kept his beautiful disposition. Many a time I looked out and saw two little children six or seven years old, sitting on the lower half of the Dutch door to his stall, eating their lunch, with Whiskey's beautiful aristocratic head leaning out over their shoulders as he shared their sandwiches.

I have mentioned these two Thoroughbreds because so many horsemen feel the Thoroughbred is unreliable, hysterical, timid, and unsuitable for use with children. Some consider him unintelligent and un-co-operative; others think he is so high-strung and overbred that he should be kept just for racing and breeding. To my mind the tremendous "heart" of the Thoroughbred, his courage and willingness to go on no matter what happens, often more than compensate for his sensitivity and nervousness. And certainly, in all the history of horses, there were never two more gallant gentlemen than Easy Going and Meadow Whisk.

Half Thoroughbred Horse Association

La Mancha, *a half bred mare, is a fine-reining stock and exhibition horse.*

The Half-bred

ORIGIN AND HISTORY

The Half-bred is an animal with one parent which is a registered Thoroughbred and the other which is not. This type of registry was started under the sponsorship of the Jockey Club which in 1919 authorized its establishment by the Genesee Valley Breeders Association. For many years the Army Remount had been interested in the promotion of the breeding of Half-breds throughout the country. They kept purebred stallions at the Remount Stations, where farmers could bring grade mares in to them. They also placed stallions out with farmers who were to charge an average of fifteen dollars as stud fee and to keep the fees thus collected. (It was from such a breeding farm that I bought Meadow Whisk, for Broom Whisk had been available in the neighborhood.) The purpose, of course, was to encourage the raising of colts of good quality which would then be available to the army.

REGISTRATION

In 1934 the American Remount Association, in whose office the work on the *Half-Bred Stud Book* had been carried on, acquired this book from the Genesee Valley Breeders Association. The American Remount Association was liquidated in June of 1952. Altogether there were three volumes of the *Half-Bred Stud Book* published—one in 1930 by the same Association and one in 1937 by the American Remount Association.

E. E. Hurlbutt, founder of the International Arabian Horse Association and its president from 1950 to 1955, acquired the Half-Arab and Anglo-Arab registries and turned these over to the Half-Thoroughbred Registry. His wife, Frances C. Hurlbutt, is the present registrar of the *Stud Book*. The address is Suite 306, 224 East Olive Avenue, Burbank, California.

TYPES AND USES

Every effort is being made to stimulate the interest in the Half-bred or, as they are called correctly, the Half-Thoroughbred. Many state colleges and agricultural schools throughout the country are maintaining Thoroughbred stallions and permitting service to grade mares for a very low stud fee. The get of these mares have proved popular for many different purposes, as Polo ponies, as Stock horses, as Hunters and Jumpers and as general-purpose animals.

Of course, there is a wide variety in type, due to the difference in types of blood lines used other than Thoroughbred. The present registry rules state that one parent, either sire or dam of the foal, must be a purebred registered Thoroughbred. The other parent may be of any other breed, purebred or not. Many of the foals are thus eligible for registry in two stud books, Half-Thoroughbred and Anglo-Arab, for example.

It is hoped that the breed can be better established eventually by limiting the registrations to foals whose dams are Half-Thoroughbred mares and whose sires are Thoroughbreds.

The Half-Thoroughbred Association welcomes inquiries and letters regarding the breed. It issues a short brochure suggesting ways in which in-

Tarrance

Meadow Lark, *son of Meadow Whisk out of Bonny*

terest in the breed can be promoted through special classes in shows, races for Half-breds, and special classes in the horse shows.

GENERAL UTILITY AND PLEASURE HORSES

My own experience has convinced me that of all modern breeds to be found in the United States, the Half-bred is one of the most satisfactory. However, one should not start with a picture of exactly what to expect in a Half-bred. The Canadian Hunter, that sagacious, sturdy, dependable animal, is very often either a Half-bred or a Three-quarter-bred. The attractive hunting pony may easily be a Half-bred with Hackney, Welsh, or other blood.

Even the get of the same stallion and mare can vary greatly. For example, we kept two foals out of Bonny, a range mare, and Meadow Whisk, who are almost completely opposite in color, build and disposition, yet both are outstanding as children's mounts.

Meadow Lark is a rather weedy fifteen-two (Bonny was fourteen-one and Whiskey, as I have stated, was fourteen-two). He has his mother's head and color but otherwise does not physically resemble either parent. He did inherit two very strong temperamental characteristics, one from his sire and the other from his dam. He has the same incredible ability to learn quickly that made Meadow Whisk such a pleasure to work with. For example, when the time came to teach him the gallop departs, in less than five minutes I taught him to break correctly into either the left or right lead, as desired, from a halt.

Bonny was a "herd leader" and would often discipline the other mares and horses, but she would never hurt a child. Lark inherited this same feeling for the safety of the rider. (I might add that he did not inherit Bonny's ideas of being responsible for the discipline of the other horse, and he has never been known to kick or bite one.) Sometimes things happen which seem to try a horse's nerves almost to the breaking point. One such incident occurred when Lark was a four-year-old: We were in the ring, and the class was trotting for the first time that day. No one realized it, but the young rider who had saddled up Lark had put a girth on him that was about two inches too long. As she came around the corner at a smart pace, she put too much weight on her inside stirrup, with the result that the saddle turned completely under the horse's belly and the rider ended up on her back, her head between the horse's back feet and her legs between his front feet.

I have seen saddles turn on horses before, and, as a rule, it scares them so much that they become completely hysterical. But Lark, realizing that a child was in danger, froze in his tracks and stood like an image until I had crossed the ring, gotten the child up and out, and released the buckle on the girth.

Today Meadow Lark is nineteen years old. He looks like a six-year-old and is still one of the most delightful mounts I have ever ridden. Bonny, who is now well in her thirties, has been retired for the past ten years but is still able and happy.

Meadow Sweet, Lark's full sister, who is now seventeen, is very different in looks and character from her brother. She is a bay, fourteen-one and one half in height. For the first ten years she was very undependable, especially over jumps. She inherited her mother's dominating character and was very free with her heels with other horses, though, like the dam, she was always quiet to handle. About five years ago Sweet settled down and has become one of our most dependable children's mounts. One of her young riders won the PHA Dressage on her in Madison Square Garden three years ago. I have used her photograph in several of my books to illustrate perfect form and type for a child's Hunter. Last year my little granddaughter came to spend the winter, and, as she was both timid and completely inexperienced she was assigned Sweet. So successful was the combination that Logan conquered her fears completely and became a competent rider. It was from Sweet I learned that an instructor should beware of "typing" his pupils and deciding how far they would go. For Logan, originally so timid, learned to jump three feet bareback without reins after only one winter, while Sweet, who used to love nothing so much as to plant any rider who did not have the delicate, sensitive hands of the expert, turned out to be an ideal nursemaid and tutor.

A five-gaited saddle horse at the rack

CHAPTER III

The Saddle Horse Division

American Saddle Horse

Of all the prominent breeds, the American Saddle Horse is the least well known outside the United States. In 1958 my friend and fox-hunting companion, Mr. C. J. Cronan, Jr., one of the directors of the American Saddle Horse Breeders Association, showed a very beautiful film in Ireland on this breed. In the audience of about a hundred people there were not only Irish men and women but English, Dutch, French and some of other nationalities. Many of these people were widely traveled and all were intensely interested in all forms of horse activities. None of them, except a few who had attended one or more big horse shows in the States, had ever seen an American Saddle Horse either in the flesh or on the screen. The pictures came as a revelation, and murmurs of surprise and admiration were heard coming from all parts of the room throughout the film. Yet, except for the racing Thoroughbred bought on the merit of his track record for breeding purposes, the American Saddle Horse is the highest-priced equine in the market today.

An amateur, waiting to compete in children's and local shows only, will have to put up a sum running well into four figures. A stable owner who plans to show his horses under professional riders and trainers in the

A three-gaited saddle horse colt

big shows will often have to go to five figures for a likely prospect, and his trainer's annual stipend will also run into five figures.

ORIGIN AND HISTORY

How did the American Saddle Horse reach these heights, and how did he ever get started in the first place? The answer begins in the seventeenth century, a hundred years before the introduction into Europe of the three famous desert stallions, founders of the English Thoroughbred. At this time there were two main classes of horses: the heavy draft animals, de-

An American saddlebred stallion, shown in fine harness

scendents of the "Great Horse" of medieval days, and the ordinary riding horse. This was before the time of even passable roads, and anyone who wanted to move more than a mile or so from home had to do so on horseback. Naturally, for journeys of any length a smooth-gaited horse was preferred. The art of "posting" or rising to the trot was not discovered until the days of the great post coaches, when the near horse of every pair was ridden by a "post boy." The trot is comfortable for the horse but much less so for the rider, especially if it is good strong trot. The trotter, therefore, was assigned to the squires and servants while the "cavalier," or gentlemen, rode a gaited horse, namely, a pacer.

The pace, or lateral gait, of most horses is very uncomfortable, as a rule—even more uncomfortable than the trot—but the "broken," or interrupted, pace, in which the two lateral legs do not strike the ground at exactly the same time, is smooth. The latter gait was preferred in England at this time, and horses with a predisposition to pacing were imported as saddle horses into the New World.

In England and on the Continent the picture changed as the eighteenth century brought an improvement in roads. Wheeled transportation became both practical and common, and speedy but powerful trotters were needed. The Hackney and the big Coach Horses became the fashion. For sport the nobleman turned to racing and to hunting, and speed at the gallop was the prime goal. With the introduction of Arabian bloodlines, the English Thoroughbred came into being. No special effort was made to develop smoothness of gaits for the average riding horse. Coaches were available for long trips, women were quite happy with their "palfries," and men wanted the Thoroughbred, with his speed and ability to jump. For short distances his trot was perfectly comfortable, for by now the post boys had discovered the knack of rising to the trot.

But in the New World, especially in Virginia and Kentucky, the horse remained the general servant of the family, to be used for daily travel, and it would be another hundred years before there were many passable roads. Race tracks were not so common or popular as they were in the North, yet the Virginia and Kentucky plantation owner needed and used horses daily. These Southern cavaliers, younger sons of aristocrats who had come to the New World to seek their fortunes, were not contented with the mild-mannered, smooth-traveling Saddler of England. They wanted something special, an animal more fitting to carry the "master of the plantation." Smooth gaits were needed, for they spent many hours in the saddle every day; but they also wanted beauty, spirit, size, and speed. A type of horse was desired that showed off well when hitched to a buggy or, as a pair, to a carriage.

How were they to develop a horse with these desired traits? The answer lay not in the introduction of one type of blood but of several. The early Thoroughbreds had the fineness and the "look of eagles." The Morgans could contribute steadiness and stamina, and the Arabian was known to improve any strain to which his blood was introduced. So, with this knowledge, the Southern cavalier started, through selective breeding, to produce a horse in his own image, an aristocrat with fire, presence, and strength.

In 1891 the first American Saddle Horse Breeders Association was formed. It listed fourteen Foundation Sires. At this time the effort to standardize the American Saddle Horse had been going on for about a hundred years. Certain "families" had been found that continued to produce the desired traits. Certain "nicks" were favored above others. This original list of fourteen was augmented to sixteen over the next seven years. Many of the horses were identified by the surname of their owners, and were as follows:

Denmark	Copperbottom
Brinker's Drennon	Stump-the-Dealer
Sam Booker	Texas
John Dillard	Prince Albert
Tom Hal	Peter's Halcorn
Coleman's Eureka	Varnon's Roebuck
Van Meter's Waxy	Davy Crockett
Cabell's Lexington	Harrison Chief

In 1902 the list was shortened to ten, the others being given ordinary registration numbers, and in 1908 all except Denmark were so reduced and the latter became the sole Foundation Sire of the American Saddle Horse breed.

Denmark was a Thoroughbred. He was mated to the Stevenson Mare, of the early colonial stock, by Cockspur, and the result was Gaines Denmark. Of today's registered Saddle Horses descending from Denmark on the male side, practically all trace back to this mating.

For the introduction of Arabian blood, Zilcadi, a desert stallion, was first crossed to a grandson of old Justin Morgan. It was found that the mare produced from this union nicked well with the Saddlers. There were other infusions of Arabian blood, but Zilcadi is one of the best-known and most successful. Other Morgan blood was introduced through breeding to members of the Black Hawk family of that breed.

Harrison Chief, a Thoroughbred, had a great propensity for speed at the trot. The Highland line, also Thoroughbred, was prominent in the Black Eagle family, antecedents of Black Squirrel; and Highland Denmark is one of the best-known of the early great Saddlers. Another well-known family is the Peavine. Tom Hal, one of the original Foundation Sires, was noted for his stamina, his longevity (he is reported to have lived to the age of forty-one), and the diversity of talent in his progeny. Bald Stockings, a son, made the running walk famous, and other horses sired by Tom Hal became noted as founders of a line of Harness Horses. Not only his sons, but his grandsons and great-grandsons as well, continued to win fame as Saddlers.

DEVELOPMENT

The American Saddle Horse was soon classified into three types: "three-gaited," "five-gaited," and "fine-harness." The neophyte at a horse show needs only to glance at the hairdos of the line of entries to know which of the first two classifications he is watching. The five-gaited aristocrats display long, bushy tails that all but sweep the ground. In fact, if nature has not been kind in this respect, the natural tail is often augmented by an "equine switch." Their manes, too, are fine and long, often hanging well down the shoulders. The foretops and first few inches behind the poll are braided with colored wool and hang in fine pigtails.

If three-gaited, the manes will be non-existent, and the artificially set tails will be plucked to mere wisps. In action, this cavalier of the horse world shows his breeding. His head is held high with the ears pricked, and with a beautiful, symmetrical curve of crest. His nose is at the vertical or slightly forward of it. His front and hind feet are lifted high, the action being straight, the soles of the feet rotating in the form of a wheel, changing their angles to face the ground, the rear, and the sky as they move.

In the five-gaited class, when the steward's long-awaited "Rack on!" rings out, the crowd holds its breath and then explodes into cheers as the champions increase their speed more and more without ever changing the rhythmical cadence of the four-beat gait. Here too is where the inbred stamina comes to light, for it is not unusual for a judge to spend an hour in judging a class, keeping the entries going around and around at this, the most tiring of gaits, in order that he may decide which horse retains his original fire and "presence" in such a test.

For those not familiar with the breed, it will be noted that the divisions of three- and five-gaited refer to the gaits required in the show ring. The three-gaited Saddler shows the flat-footed walk, the trot, and the canter. The five-gaited horse must show, in addition to these gaits, a "slow-gait," and a "rack." The latter is often called a "single-foot," since only one foot at a time is placed on the ground. This same is also true of the "slow-gait."

FINE HARNESS

In the Fine Harness and "Combination" classes (in which the five-gaited Saddler is first shown to an appropriate vehicle and unharnessed, then saddled up in the ring and ridden), one can live vicariously in the exciting age when fine ladies and gentlemen drove to their engagements behind one or more of these beauties. There will never be an automobile made which will approach the glamor of a well-turned-out vehicle, whether it be a buggy, ladies' phaeton, carriage-and-pair, or four-in-hand, all common sights before the replacement of the blacksmith shop by the garage.

AS A SHOW HORSE

With its valuable purses and trophies, the American Horse Show has most certainly been the prime factor in the breeding and development of today's Show Saddler. This animal is a professional in every sense of the word. He is trained and lives for one thing only—to compete successfully against his peers in the show ring. His shoeing, his feeding, and his handling are all aimed at this one goal.

The first and foremost quality he must show is "animation"—fire, flash, and "presence." No matter how high he may step, or how well he may carry himself, without this "presence" to catch the judge's eye, his career as a successful show animal is doomed. With a huge sum of money at stake, is it any wonder that some practices used to produce this air of animation and considered legitimate appear to other horsemen not only completely artificial but cruel? Yet, against competition, the trainer who does not use these methods would have great difficulty in winning. Of course some trainers go much further than others in the use of the whip before entering the ring to insure alertness and a spirited entrance. Not all trainers insist that the Show Saddler must be treated as a machine and never as a pet or friend, but the majority of them do.

Next to "presence," or animation, comes the demand for high action and lofty carriage of head and tail. The horse that carries his head high, with a well-flexed crest and jaw, and goes "on the bit" with his center of gravity over his own center, is a far more comfortable mount than one that "goes on his forehand." A naturally high-set tail is supposed to denote strenth of back. Docking of Hunters and driving horses was common everywhere in the seventeenth, eighteenth, and nineteenth centuries. Docking the hunter prevented his tail getting caught in the blackthorn hedges, common obstacles in the English hunt field. One of the grave dangers in driving occurs when a horse gets his tail over the rein and clamps it down. Some horses develop this habit as a vice, and as soon as the driver finds himself helpless (for pulling on the remaining rein would lead to catastrophe), the animal either bolts or kicks the rig to pieces. Young horses sometimes could be rendered hysterical when, by accident, they felt the rein under their tails. So, practically all Harness horses were docked, and even today the Hackneys are so treated.

It was only a step from "docking" the tail to "setting" it so that it would always be held high. Horses whose tails have been operated on for this permanently lose the normal use of their tails to keep away insects and must have the altered appendage kept in a type of special harness called a "tail-set." Some states have gone so far as to outlaw this practice. Each year at the National Horse Show the American Society for Prevention of Cruelty to Animals (ASPCA) threatens to bar the exhibiting of such animals in the ring, but each year they still appear. The exponents of tail setting say that with his extremely high-head carriage the Saddler would look unbalanced and ridiculous with a normal tail and that a horse kept properly protected from flies does not need a tail to keep them off. It is true that we have become so used to looking at these artificially held tails that anything else would appear peculiar. But the same thing was true in the days when it was considered fashionable to trim the ears of Thoroughbreds in order to make them look more "refined."

But it is not enough to operate on the tail. Everyone in the Saddle-horse world agrees that the use of ginger is a must for show horses. This is chewed and placed in the anus to act as an irritant, and causes the horse to appear mettlesome and hold his tail even higher. We cannot blame this practice on the lovers of the breed, however. Surtees refers quite often to dealers' use of ginger in this way to make their animals look more high-spirited, and a famous nightmare attributed to one of his characters is that of a dealer who dreamed that he saw an affluent and reliable customer coming and couldn't lay hands on the ginger!

The exaggeratedly high action necessary for Saddlers is the result of several factors. Breeders select mares and stallions that demonstrate this characteristic; they grow the hoofs as long as possible, weight the shoes, and use light chains or wooden rollers fastened loosely around the pastern in training. None of these practices can be called cruel; in fact, such a strain is put on the walls and tendons that, of necessity, the American Saddle Horse has developed tremendously strong legs and feet.

So much for the physical characteristics necessary to make a successful show champion. Add to these intelligence, docility, a willingness and ability to learn, and we have a potential winner. But he will never win in good company without a first-class professional to train and probably to show him. The horse must be balanced under his rider, and ridden on the bit, so that the rider has complete control of every step he takes. The position of the rider, way back on the cantle to show off his horse's front, might be criticized as not having any basically sound principles of equitation to back it up. However, the sensitivity of the rider's hands and his complete control cannot be denied. He must demand just enough impulsion to be balanced by collection. He must feel just what the horse is doing under him and also what he may do, interpreting what the animal feels and encouraging or discouraging it. He and his horse together form a part of a machine whose one purpose is to go into the ring and win. It has taken three hundred years to develop this machine and its perfection as such cannot be denied.

Outside The Show Ring

Turning from the show animal, we must consider the American Saddle Horse as a type of individual. What is he good for besides the show ring? What has he done in the past outside of providing his master or mistress with a desirable, worthy mount? What use can he be today for those who haven't the money, the experience, or the desire to keep a stable of fine animals just for the purpose of showing them?

As we have seen, the Saddler is exceptionally strong and hardy, not only in his legs and feet but also in his back and his general stamina. His well-developed chest and well-sprung rib cage give him a barrrel with plenty of room for his heart, lungs, and other organs. A well set-on head, clean-cut throttle, and wide flaring nostrils provide those characteristics necessary for a strong respiratory system.

Temperamentally he is high-strung and sensitive, but he lacks the tendency toward foolish hysteria and sudden explosions that plagues many Thoroughbreds. He retains the hot-blooded horse's impulse to move out rather than balk when things do not go to his liking or when he is confused. In fact, he is one of the least stubborn of the equines and often seems to have a special place in his heart for children.

American saddle horse and buggy in Aiken, South Carolina

KOROSCO B

The only purebred American Saddle Horse I ever owned was a retired stallion named Korosco B, which I bought in the early 1930's. He was five-gaited and fourteen years old at the time. We had an old, rather tumbledown barn in those days, with one box stall and three or four straight stalls. Korosco, of course, was immediately assigned the box, and its former tenant, a registered Hambletonian named Ariel, was demoted to one of the straight stalls. I can truthfully say I have never met a finer equine gentleman than Korosco B. When I appeared at his stall door, he would leave the window through which he liked to watch the passing traffic and come over to me at once. Seeing the bridle hung over my arm he would obligingly lower his head, push it through the cavesson and open his mouth to receive the bit.

When I first mounted, he invariably started showing off, sashaying around as though walking on hot coals, and piaffing. I say invariably, but this did not hold true if I took my a year-and-a-half old son up in front of me. The instant the child was lifted into place, even though it might be before

Saddle horses hitched to a London coach

the old stallion had had time to have his fun, he would voluntarily step out calmly and quietly.

SQUIRREL

When I bought Korosco B, I also bought his unbroken two-year-old son, out of a mare that was part Saddle and part Trotter. Since the Black Squirrel family was predominent in his ancestry, I named the colt Bay Squirrel.

Squirrel inherited his father's habit of approaching, lowering his head, and opening his mouth for the bit when he saw the bridle. There are the only two horses I have ever known that had this particular habit. I have always ·wondered how the experts on heredity would explain it.

Squirrel also inherited his father's tenderness with little children. When he had been in the stable only a week or so, and before we had begun any formal training, he scratched his leg on a wall in the pasture and the wound became infected. It was on the near hind leg, and from hock to ankle-joint that member was swollen over twice its normal size. Naturally, too, it was

An American saddle horse jumping

exceedingly sensitive. In fact, I could barely run my hand down Squirrel's gaskin without having him flinch in apprehension. Yet if I were to help it, I had first to bathe it for a period of at least a half hour in hot water and Epsom salts and then apply a hot wet dressing. I was alone then, without stable help.

I cross-tied the colt on the barn floor, went to the house, and came back with the hot water, Epsom salts, and a suitable tub. Then, as gently as possible, I started to work. Although I talked and soothed and coaxed, the pain was too great. The minute the dripping towel touched any part of the affected leg Squirrel jumped and danced, lifting the leg, stamping it, and moving as much as the side ties would permit.

I continued talking and trying. Somehow I *had* to get him to submit, painful as I knew it to be. I was crouched, facing the rear and opposite the front of his sore leg when suddenly he stopped fidgeting and stood like a rock.

"Good," I thought, "he's made up his mind to put up with it, and now we'll get somewhere." Gently and slowly I ran the hot towel down to the hock and let the water run down the leg. Squirrel flinched but did not move his leg.

"Brave boy," I said with satisfaction, thanking whatever Providence was responsible for his sudden change of behavior. But it was not a kind Providence. It was Squirrel's own hereditary instinct that had caused his sudden quietness. For, looking over my shoulder, I saw my little son standing directly under the horse's belly calmly eating an apple! The colt had endured the pain and restrained himself for fear of hurting the child. When the boy was out of the way, he went back to his restlessness, but now the heat had begun to take effect, the pain was not so severe, and he was able to associate my ministrations with something designed to help him. With both of us doing our best I was able not only to bathe the limb thoroughly but also to persuade Squirrel to let me put the injured leg into the tub where it could soak.

Needless to say, with this type of intelligence and willingness, Squirrel soon became one of our most treasured and reliable mounts. He easily developed both the slow-gait and the rack and he had the most delightful "rocking-chair" canter I have ever ridden. As a child in Virginia the description of a desirable saddle horse that could "canter all day under the shade of a tree" had always been familiar, and Squirrel certainly typified that expression! Because of his gentleness and his smoothness of gait, he soon became known as the "invalid's and mother's delight," for pregnant women and victims of hunting accidents still wearing casts could ride him in perfect safety and comfort.

Squirrel had other talents as well. When my oldest daughter was about seven, she was very anxious to show in the children's Hunter classes in the little local shows. In those days few young children rode in shows at all, and the classes were not divided according to age or size of mount. All jumps were three feet or higher. Shirley was a good little rider and used to go hunting with us on her pony, Old Jess. But the latter was a ten-hand, twenty-year-old Shetland and could hardly be expected to measure up to these standards.

"When we have a suitable mount, you shall certainly show in both the Hunter and Jumper classes," I told the child, and thought no more about the matter. Squirrel, at the time, was a nine-year-old, and, being a gaited horse, no one had bothered to teach him to jump. Yet it was only a few weeks later that Shirley announced she had found her Hunter and wanted to enter him in the approaching Wilton Show.

"Who is it?" I asked wondering what neighbor had been persuaded to supply her with a mount.

"Squirrel."

"But, he doesn't jump!"

"He does now!"

I went out to see. Sure enough, Squirrel took anything she put him at, calmly and carefully!

The day of the show came, along with the first attempt on the part of both horse and rider at competition over an outside course. In this one the contestants were required to line up inside the ring. Then, one at a time, they were asked to leave the line, jump out over a designated panel, turn right, canter down a steep, trappy grade and over another bar, turn again to the right, and return on the course proper which was laid in a big circle. The eight obstacles included a couple of hedges, a snake fence, and an in-and-out. The entry then galloped down another slope, turned to the left, came up the original rise over the second bar, and then jumped back into the ring. Neither Shirley nor Squirrel had ever before ridden over such a course or seen a hedge, a snake fence, or an in-and-out. Shirley's class was not scheduled until the afternoon, so, during the luncheon period, we tried out the course. Everything went smoothly and both the child and the horse seemed both cool and confident.

"I have only one piece of advice to give you," I said as they were standing at the in-gate. "*Walk* into the ring to line up. When your turn comes, leave

Shirley Self rides Squirrel.

the line at a walk and line up opposite the first jump and halt. When you get the signal to proceed, pick up the canter from the *halt*, don't take any trotting steps, as he just might stick in a few steps of the rack or the slow-gait. When you jump back into the ring, come right down to the walk from the canter, preferably when the judge isn't looking!"

Since this was a children's class, it was judged 60 per cent on manners and smoothness. And manners and smoothness were what Squirrel showed. Shirley obeyed my instructions implicitly. She brought him in on a flat-footed walk. When her turn came, she walked him calmly out of the line. (This had been the downfall of many of the other young competitors whose horses, more stubborn by nature than Squirrel, rebelled at having to leave their companions.) She halted, then picked up his beautiful, rocking-chair canter and headed for the panel. From there on she left it entirely up to the horse. Taking a firm grip of the mane with both hands, she concentrated on staying on him. Squirrel did not fail her. Having been around the course once, he knew just what was expected of him. He took every obstacle in the exact center without varying his stride and jumped back into the ring as quietly as he had left it. Shirley then picked up the reins, and when she saw the Judge begin to write on his score sheet, she brought him down to a halt. Needless to say they won the blue. But the story is not finished. After she had received the ribbon and the cup and the judge had congratulated her—she was the youngest competitor by eight years—Shirley picked up her reins and left the ring at a smart rack! I saw Judge Homer Grey give her an odd look, but of course it was too late to change his opinion.

But don't think he forgot! Ten years later I met Homer Grey at the Golds Dragoons Show in Westport, Connecticut, where some of my pupils were giving an exhibition. It was a formation ride in which eight riders entered at the canter and, while cantering, removed their saddles, and then went over a series of jumps bareback with their reins knotted and their arms held shoulder high. Squirrel was one of the horses. Homer came over after the exhibition to congratulate the young riders, some of whom had hunted with him. He went over to old Squirrel and looked him over carefully.

"I remember this fellow," he said. "He's the five-gaited Saddler that fooled me into giving him a Hunter ribbon ten years ago!"

I have told these two little stories to illustrate the intelligence, kindness, amiability, and versatility of the American Saddle Horse. Indeed, he has been proven in many fields. He has been used for range work and for dressage.

Joe Aleshire, whose father was Red McDonald, son of old Rex McDonald, was a member of the U. S. Army Three Day Event team in the Olympics. In the Civil War when Army officers provided their own mounts, practically all of the Confederate horses were mostly, if not entirely, Saddle-bred, and all have heard the fame of Lee's cavalry.

Tennessee Walking Horse

ORIGIN AND HISTORY

The Tennessee Walking Horse is sometimes known as the Plantation Walker. Developed in the central basin of Tennessee, these horses trace their origin to much the same sources as the American Saddle Horse. That is, they have Thoroughbred, Morgan, American Saddle, and Standardbred blood, as well as a good deal of Canadian and Narragansett Pacing blood. Originally they were developed to provide the plantation owner with a comfortable mount, one on which he could sit all day without being tired. Straight gaits were necessary so that the owner might ride between the rows of corn or other crops without damage. Speed and the extreme animation and "presence" desired in the Saddler were not essential, although good looks, fineness, and sturdy conformation were certainly desirable. At the time of the Civil War a type of Saddle Horse known for its "free and easy" gaits was well established in both North Carolina and Tennessee. In fact, one of the outstanding stallions was called Free and Easy and was sent from Tennessee to North Carolina for stud purposes. Other well-known families or "strains" which contributed to the development of the Walking Horse were the Copperbottoms, McMeen's Traveler (by one of the original Foundation Saddle Horse sires, Stump-the-Dealer), Tom Hal, and the family of Stonewalls that came from the Denmark-Cockspur line. It is said that McMeen's Traveler sired forty-seven of the horses used in General Forest's cavalry, and that not one of these was lost during the Civil War.

In 1935 the Tennessee Walking Horse Breeders Association was organized, and a thorough search of pedigrees was made to decide which stallion had contributed the most toward the establishment of the breed. Allen F-1, a black horse with white markings, foaled in 1886, was chosen. He had a record both as a trotter and a pacer, and through his sire was descended from the Standardbreds. His great-grandsire was George Wilkes, out of Hambletonian.

The Tennessee Walking Horse poses.

His dam was of the best Narragansett Pacing blood, and her pedigree traced back through the Black Hawk family to the Morgans.

Allon F.1 sired many fine colts, among which the most outstanding were Merrylegs, Roan Allen, and Hunters Allen.

As a Show Horse

The Tennessee Walker, considered at first just a utility and pleasure horse, has now come to the fore as a show horse as well. In the ring he is required to show three gaits only, the flat-footed walk, the running walk, and the canter. His flat-footed walk must be strong, active, and evenly cadenced. The running walk is what is known as a "four-cornered gait," as opposed to a lateral gait. As in the fox-trot, or broken trot, the diagonal legs follow each

A trainer exercises Zha Zha, *winner of the Tennessee Walking Horse Amateur Class, 1963, in Kansas City, Missouri.*

other; but whereas in the latter gait the horse first plants (let us say) his right hind foot, followed an instant later by his left forefoot, in the running-walk the forefoot is planted before the hind foot. Of course in the broken pace the lateral legs follow each other in sequence, giving a rolling gait completely different from the square, four-cornered gait of the Walker. One of the outstanding characteristics of the running walk is the tremendous over-reach, the print of the back foot sometimes being as much as twenty-four inches in front of that of the forefoot on the same side. Another characteristic is the pronounced swinging of the head at each step.

The Tennessee Walking Horse wears a full mane and tail, the latter usually set and often augmented with a "switch" of false hair. He is generally shown in an English saddle and a special curb bit with long shanks.

Nevertheless, the Tennessee Walker is best known as the world's most delightful pleasure horse. He is the perfect mount for the rider who wants to go out on the trails and have a smooth comfortable ride on a willing, intelligent, good-natured animal, one that is never stubborn, never balky, never "heavy" or pulling. He completely refutes the ideas of some people who think that all horses are stupid, vicious, not to be trusted and can be handled only through fear. The Tennessee Walker resembles the man who originated him, the easy-going Southern planter, a gentleman who was a man of his word, who liked the good things of life but did not care about becoming the "best" in commercial competition. His life was regulated to an easy pace, he got along well with his neighbors, and his horse did and still does the same.

Breeding Associations

For those who would like to learn more about the breeds mentioned in this section, I include the address of the breeding associations. Both these associations have interesting publications which discuss the history, showing, and training of their respective animals. The addresses are as follows: American Saddle Horse Breeders' Association, Louisville, Kentucky; Tennessee Walking Horse Breeders' and Exhibitors' Association of America, Lewisburg, Tennessee.

CHAPTER IV

Standardbred Division

The Standardbred

Origin and History

As we have seen, the noun "Thoroughbred," to denote a specific breed of horse, is derived from the adjective "thoroughbred," meaning purebred or of pure blood. The term "Standardbred," on the other hand, denotes a horse that may be registered if he comes up to a certain standard of speed, regardless of ancestry. Originally, to be registered in the United States Trotting Registry a Harness Racer was required to trot a mile in two minutes and thirty seconds or, if he were a Pacer, two minutes and twenty-five seconds. Since those early days, the registration requirements have changed. A horse may still be registered if he meets the required standards, but he may also be registered on his pedigree just as with the Thoroughbred and other registries.

Of all American breeds, certainly the Standardbred has had one of the most varied and interesting histories. Climate, military needs, fashion, and religion all have been important factors in its development. In the South the Roadster was of no use in winter, for the few roads there became impassable bogs. This was not so in the Northeast and in Canada, for here hardpacked snow made ideal footing. The light cavalry provided a market for horses

U.S. Trotting Association Photo

Greyhound, *the world's fastest trotter*

which could trot for long distances and break readily into a gallop. But, of all factors, religion was the most important. The Puritans' blue laws forbade racing, and in 1802 all running tracks were closed. Long before that date racing had been frowned upon, and running horses, i.e., Thoroughbreds, were not favored by the New England countrymen of Puritan stock.

However, most farmers had a "roadster" which pulled the family surrey on Sunday, carried the farmer to market in his cart on week days, and worked in the plow at other times. He was not a very beautiful animal, this Roadster, but he was sturdy and fast. In 1788 a flea-bitten gray stallion, a running horse that had raced in England, was imported to be used as a stud. His name was Messenger. To the surprise of many people, his colts seemed to have an unusual propensity at the trot, perhaps because Messenger was a direct descendant of the Darley Arabian. In time certain horse families became known as Natural Roadsters, and many of these went back to Messenger. In Vermont there was the Black Hawk family. Then there were the descendants of Ethan Allen, Mambrino Chief, Henry Clay, Justin Morgan, and, above all, Rysdyk's Hambletonian.

TYPE, CONFORMATION, AND ACTION

What are the contracts between the Standardbreds and the Thorough-breds from which they are descended? The chief difference is in the general proportions. For years the Thoroughbred has been bred for length of leg without undue length of body. The powerful, pistonlike action of the trotter was supposed to depend largely on a powerful and well-developed hindquar-ter attached to a long back. Early horses, including Hambletonian and Ab-dullah, were longer than they were high, although this requirement was dis-proved by the fact that Greyhound is taller than he is long.

The movement of a Racing Trotter at the trot is very different from that

Scotch Rhythm *was one of the outstanding candidates for the Hambletonian Stake in 1951.*

Wide World Photo

Standardbred horse hitched up to a "Jet Age" sulky

of any other breed. Ordinarily when a saddler, Thoroughbred, or other type of horse is at the trot, the print of the back foot covers or is slightly ahead of, and in line with, the print of the front foot. Not so with the Roadster. The Standardbred must have a much longer stride with a tremendous overreach if he is to beat any records. To accomplish this without cutting himself to pieces, he spreads his hind legs, and his back prints are well ahead of and outside of his front prints.

TEMPERAMENT AND USE

In disposition the Standardbred, both Trotter and Pacer, is not nearly as temperamental and nervous as the Thoroughbred. He is far from being a phlegmatic animal, however, and has none of the stubborness of some of the other breeds. His stable manners are usually good, he is easy to handle and

Robert Talbot II, U.S. Trotting Association

Adios Butler, *the world's fastest pacer, finishes a mile time trial.*

makes a good riding horse once he has learned to canter slowly. This latter is difficult, since for generations he has been bred to trot, and trot only.

Trotters

Mention has been made of Messenger the Thoroughbred, foundation sire of all types of Standardbreds including Trotters, Pacers, and Roadsters. And, as has been shown, many families have contributed to the development of the racing Standardbred. Of these the name of one sire stands out as being the most important—Rysdyk's Hambletonian.

This line begins with an ugly, ungainly, bad-tempered, and thoroughly unpopular stallion named Abdullah. Abdullah was an unaccountable throwback, for he was bred to the purple, going back through the Mambrino line to Messenger. In spite of his royal blood the local farmers would not breed to him, and he became the property of Jonas Seely, a well-to-do farmer in

Orange County. Seely had a crippled mare which he had bought out of pity. She was by Bellfounder out of One Eye. One Eye had been a favorite of Seely's father, and when Seely found the daughter, permanently lamed from an accident, being used to pull a butcher's cart, he bought her and bred her to Abdullah. She is known as the Kent Mare. She, too, had outstanding blood-lines, but when she dropped her foal in 1849, Seely didn't think much of it and sold mare and foal to his hired man Bill Rysdyk for one hundred and twenty-five dollars. Actually, all he got was a "promise to pay," for the hired man had no cash.

Nevertheless, Rysdyk had enough faith in his purchase to retire and set up as a breeder. He named the foal Hambletonian, for he had the blood of Bishop's Hambletonian, another descendant of Messenger, in his veins. The foal was a powerful but ugly horse. As a two-year-old he managed to win the first prize for the best two-year-old stallion at the Orange County Fair, and the following year won five dollars as the best three-year-old stallion. But he was still not looked on as anything that might, in time, set the world on fire. In spite of his homeliness however, Rysdyk found him some mares, and three years later his get began to win on the tracks.

Time went on, and the colts and fillies sired by the ugly but powerful Rysdyk's Hambletonian continued to win. Finally, at the age of twelve, his prepotency to pass along speed at the trot was universally recognized. Today all the country's fastest Trotters and many of the Pacers trace directly back to this horse. For four generations all the antecedents of Greyhound, the world's fastest Trotter with a record of a mile trotted in 1:55-$\frac{1}{4}$, are direct descendants of the crippled Kent Mare and the unpopular Abdullah.

ARIEL

When my husband and I were first married, we bought a two-year-old filly descended from Rysdyk's Hambletonian and kept her in a community garage in South Orange, New Jersey.

I had never before ridden a Standardbred, and it was a revelation. There was a disused trolley track which ran down South Orange Avenue in those days, and I used it as my "speedway" on my way to the trails in Orange Mountain Reservation. How that mare could step out! I can still feel those powerful strides under me. She was one of the most intelligent horses I have ever known, the kind that can literally read your mind. Later, when we moved to Connecticut, we had fields in which to turn her out. This she appreciated and was sometimes extremely reluctant to be caught, especially if it meant work. She always knew when I wanted her for the latter purpose and when I was just coming up to her to pat her or give her a tidbit. Even though, in the former case, I used the same tone of voice and carried no rope, she still knew the difference and would high-tail it across the meadow as soon as I approached.

She was a sensible horse. Once in South Orange I happened to be opposite the firehouse when the fire siren went off. In those days they still had firehorses. I waited for the few seconds required, and when they dashed out and took off up the avenue, I was right at their heels at the trot on my "speedway." So exhilarated was I that I paid no attention to the footing until I felt Ariel give a tremendous spring and leap a distance of at least fifteen feet. Only automatic reaction kept me in the saddle. A glance back over my shoulder showed that, unknown to me, the town had excavated the width of the trolley tracks for a distance of about eight feet in order to uncover a sewer pipe. Had Ariel been as unobservant and careless as I, it would probably have been disastrous for us both.

It took me three years to teach Ariel to take up a slow canter, partly because of her indisposition to canter slowly, but mainly because I didn't know how to go about it. One brisk winter day, however, she learned out of necessity. We had had a week of bad weather ending with an icestorm. I brought her out to give her a little airing, intending to keep at the walk. But Ariel would have none of walking. She wanted to race. I kept vibrating the reins to keep her in check and to my delight she went into a beautiful rocking-chair canter. From then on it was easy. She and I had finally learned to talk "horse language" together. I later found that she had a natural very rapid rack which she would take from an extended trot. Her tremendous spring over the excavation had already taught me that she could jump, so I had long since begun training her for the hunt field. I also found a Hempsted cart and broke her to harness. Now she was really in her element, with only one fault—she couldn't bear to stand still. She would stop readily enough if I wanted to speak to a passerby, but I had about thirty seconds to say what I wanted, and then she would be off, regardless of my wishes.

Ariel lived well into her twenties. We bred her several times to old Korosko B, our Saddle stallion, but none of her colts approached the mother or father in quality, so evidently it was not a successful "nick." Ariel is a horse I will always remember.

Pacers

The normal trot is a diagonal gait, the right forefoot and left hind foot striking the ground almost simultaneously, followed by the alternate diagonal. In the pace the horses' lateral legs move at the same time (right hind and fore, for example) and hence the nickname, "sidewheeler." The pace is slightly faster than the trot. The world's record for a mile, set by Greyhound in 1938, was 1:55-1/4, and that for pacing, set in 1960 by Adios Butler, is 1:54-3/5. Why, then, for so many years was trotting so much more popular than pacing, with many more Trotters being trained than Pacers? The answer

Wide World Photo

Pacing harness horses are trained at Pinehurst Race Track, North Carolina.

lies in the fact that though there were many horses with a predisposition to pacing there were very few that could be depended on not to break. In harness racing, when a horse breaks from the trot or pace into a gallop, this does not disqualify him, but he must immediately be pulled back, taken to the outside and started again on the desired gait. When a Trotter breaks, this is accomplished easily, for he can shift gears, so to speak, from the trot to the gallop and back to the trot without difficulty. On the contrary, the Pacer has difficulty breaking from the gallop back into the pace.

However, in 1885 a railroad conductor named John Browning invented a type of leg harness called "hopples" which made it impossible for the horse to move his legs in any sequence other than laterally. At first objections were raised that the use of hopples constituted an infringement of the no-artificial-aids rule, but later they were permitted, and today all Pacers wear them.

There have been many famous Pacing Horses, a few of whom are Dan Patch, Single G, Billy Direct, and Adios Butler. The latter was bought in 1955 for five hundred thousand dollars, and later, in 1960, he was syndicated for six hundred thousand.

For general riding purposes the Pacer is not so comfortable as the Trotter. It is said that the old Narragansett Pacer, a breed which has disappeared, had a comfortable gait under the saddle, but, generally speaking, the rolling motion of the pace, impossible for posting, is uncomfortable in the extreme.

Standardbred Racing

A study of the breed of horse known as Standardbred would be incomplete if, in addition to searching out their origin, present-day type, and use, we failed to take into consideration the enormous influence that racing at the trot and pace, either for fun, for glory, or for a purse, has had on the development and preservation of the breed.

Competition is a deeply imbedded instinct in the human race, and when, in 1802, all racetracks for running horses were closed on religious principles, the sportsman turned to Harness Horses. For it was contended that a race was a contest to see who could cover a given distance in the shortest time. This being so, if a horse were trotting or pacing, he obviously was not going as fast as he could. Strictly speaking, therefore, this was not a race and so was not banned.

Up until 1823 all races were on "speedways" (roads or streets set aside for this purpose) or on fairgrounds. Most of the contests were under saddle. Occasionally there would be endurance rides or races, the route from New York to Boston being one.

The first speedway in Manhattan was in the Bowery. Later, on Long Island, addicts of the sport used the Jamaica Road. Most of the drivers were amateurs. Trotting horses had caught on with the fashionable set by now, and it was the vogue to appear in the afternoon with one's fleetest horse and ride up and down these speedways, inviting competition and winning plaudits from the fair sex who, as might be expected, would appear in the latest "Godey's Print" costumes and cheer from the sidelines. But these roads were also open to ordinary traffic, and when the amateur contests became too fast and furious, many complaints were lodged. As a result, in 1807 Third Avenue was laid out for the express purpose of providing a straightaway to take the speedsters off the other roads.

Beginning about 1830, trotting races under saddle became less popular, and the interest switched to driving. What was known as "barnstorming" or "hippodroming" was especially popular. This was the running of races at local tracks for a purse in connection with a fair or other event. Trotting "circuits" also came into favor. Among the earliest Trotters to go on circuit were Flora Temple and Lancet, who toured the country racing against each other for a purse and a share of the gate receipts. Later, Flora Temple went on alone and raced against the local horses at Detroit, Chicago, Kalamazoo, Sondersby, Adrian, and St. Louis. Another type of race was entered by Tom Thumb, who

Stenographer, a trotter, was named Harness Horse of the Year by the U.S. Trotting Association in 1954.

Wide World Photo

was shipped to England, where he trotted a hundred miles over a five-mile course. This occurred on February 2, 1829, and his time was ten hours and seven minutes.

However, there was no way of controlling these early races, and between 1830 and 1850 trotting races lost popularity with the society set. For one thing, the Church frowned on it, and also ladies refused to attend because of rowdyism.

Nevertheless, amateur speedsters were not to be kept under for long, and an album of Currier and Ives prints clearly shows the comeback of the sport, especially in New York City. Two of the most famous gentlemen drivers of that era were Robert Bonner, millionaire owner of the New York Ledger, and Commodore Cornelius Vanderbilt. For a period of about ten years they challenged each other to "brushes" on the speedways. As soon as one man found himself being consistently defeated by the other, he set out at once to find swifter horses. Vanderbilt did his best to get Bonner to compete for a

A roadster pulls a light sulky.

Carl Klein Photo

purse of ten thousand dollars in a race where he would drive his matched pair, Plow Boy and Post Boy, against Bonner's pair of mares, Lady Palmer and Flatbush Maid. But Bonner was a strict churchman and would not race for money.

Bonner would not admit defeat, either. He waited until Vanderbilt was present with his horses at a race at the fashion course. When the day's events were over, he offered to race his mares against time, simply to show that he could beat the day's record of 2:31-1/4. This he did, lowering that day's record for the mile trotted by a pair by two full seconds. Then he offered to give ten thousand dollars to any gentleman who could beat that record. But Vanderbilt could not accept the challenge, as no gentleman could accept such a gift should he win.

Late in the 1860's, trotting racing again fell into disrepute, due to swindling, rowdyism, and the impossibility of exerting any sort of discipline or control at the tracks. Obviously some sort of organization was needed that could exert this discipline and, at the same time, organize the sport in such a way that the owners and trainers would find it worth their while to compete and the breeders would find a ready and profitable market. The latter in turn would insure the improvement of the breed.

In 1870 such a Trotting Association was formed, to be followed by the National Trotting Association of today. This 1870 association had its hands full of problems, but it was a success from the start.

One of the most complicated problems was just how to decide the records. In those days all the sulkies had high wheels and were difficult to pull around the sharp turns of the oval track. Then someone thought of building a track in the shape of a kite. Sure enough, it was found that on these tracks the time was definitely diminished. But how were the horses to be classified? How could a horse that had a record of 2:31 on a Kite Track be classified when racing on an ordinary oval track? There were also other methods being used in the same period. For example, in racing against time, a Trotter would sometimes have a Running Horse hitched to a sulky carrying a sail in front of him and another horse on each side to "box him in" and cut down the wind resistance. How did these affect his record? Obviously, horses needed to be handicapped just as Running Horses are handicapped. The Harness Horse could not be handicapped by weight, so he had to be classified according to his record. This meant that once a horse had trotted at a record speed he could no longer find anyone to race against until others had made a

A road hack displays his trot under saddle at a horse show.

similar record. The result was that drivers pulled their horses, and the racing was stultified.

The matinees and fairs were all very fine but the purses were not large enough. In 1873 the Grand Circuit was organized by the Trotting Association. It had four member tracks with a total of $170,000 in prize money. Today there are more than fifty tracks on the Grand Circuit, and the purses amount to over $4,000,000.

The shape of the track was solved by the advent of the low-wheeled sulky, an import from England. And how the crowds hooted the first day it appeared on a track! It was used once in the morning and twice in the afternoon. The drivers (Ed Geers first, and then the renowned Budd Doble) not only won all three races but lowered the world's record. The sulky with the bicycle wheels was here to stay.

It was not until the 1940's that harness racing appeared on a pari-mutuel basis. The first was at the Roosevelt Raceway on Long Island. This has now become an outstanding attraction in all parts of the country. However, it has not cut out the smaller tracks and fairs, for harness racing still draws an annual crowd of an estimated nine million spectators at the smaller tracks alone.

Two things, besides the enormous increase in the purses, have been responsible for this tremendous mushrooming of the sport. One was the handicapping by amounts of money won rather than on time. The other was the starting gate. Beginning with the sum of two hundred dollars, horses now race against their peers classified as to those who have not won the above amount, those that have not won four hundred dollars, seven hundred dollars, etc., until we get to non-winners of fifty thousand dollars. All horses that have won fifty thousand dollars or more are considered to be in the same class and race each other.

The invention of the starting gate has changed the original system of racing for the better. Up until only a few years ago, the contestants were brought out on the track, warmed up by trotting "clockwise," and then they all turned and headed for the starting line. They had to cross this line abreast before the word "go," indicating that the race could start. Sometimes this took as much as a half hour, and meanwhile the crowd became restive. Then in 1946, a mechanical gate with wings which formed a barrier was mounted on the back of a moving car. The field could now be held in line until all were trotting, and then the gate pulled out of the way. A success from the first, this gate has since been improved upon and is used at all major tracks and most minor ones.

A second improvement in the system of racing is that of having a single "dash" instead of the same horses racing in several "heats" to decide the winner. In one afternoon there will be several of these "dashes" with different contestants in each, just as in other types of racing. Thus the spectators do not see the same contestants again and again, and the strain on the horses is not as great.

Mention should also be made of the biggest races held each year, those which have the same significance to the harness racer that has the Kentucky Derby, the Preakness, etc., have for the follower of the Runners.

For trotters there is first and foremost the famed Hambletonian Race. Sponsored by the Hambletonian Society, it was first raced at Syracuse in 1926, and is for three-year-olds. In 1957 the location was moved to Du Quoin, Illinois, where it is still being held. In 1960 the purse was over $144,560.

For three-year-olds we also have the Kentucky Futurity (a futurity is a race for which the foal is nominated before birth), held in Lexington, Kentucky, and the Yonkers Futurity held on the Yonkers Raceway.

So much for the "big time." But, unlike the picture of Thoroughbred racing, there are still many old-time trainers and drivers whose love is for owning, training, and driving one or possibly two fast-stepping Roadsters. Dressed in the gay racing silks, and omitting only the handle-bar mustaches of their fathers, they race against their neighbors at fairs and carnivals, more for an inherent interest in the sport than for the money to be won.

The Roadster

We come now to the Roadster division and the types of classes offered in the Horse Shows. The most picturesque, of course, is Roadsters driven to sulkies. Nothing is much more thrilling than to see these skillful drivers, usually older men, hanging out on the side of the light little sulkies, long driving whips in hand, as they cut the corners of the tight oval of an ordinary show ring in an effort to get on the inside. One also has the feeling that these men are not just professional trainers, working because they are paid to. They train and drive because they love it. The Roadster is gone from the country roads, from Harlem Lane and Third Avenue. Harness racing has become big time, but, contrary to the Runners, there is still a place for the

one- or two-horse owner-driver who keeps his racer in a small barn and shows
or races his horse himself.

There are also classes in some shows for the so-called Road Hacks ridden under saddle, with 60 per cent being awarded for speed and the trot.
One sees fewer and fewer of these classes, and, though exciting to watch,
they are not so popular as the classes for the high-stepping Saddlers.

CHAPTER V

Western Division

Mustangs

ORIGIN AND HISTORY

Ancestors of the true wild horses of the West, the Mustangs, were the Spanish horses introduced into Mexico by Cortes and later into other parts of North and South America by the conquistadores. These horses were of Arabian ancestry and many were Andalusians. There were horses of every color including the so-called Ysabellas, horses with a solid body color and flaxen-colored manes and tail. They are so named because Queen Isabella of Spain was the first to have a matched horse bodyguard of this marking. They range from the deep-chocolate and liver chestnut to the palominos. There must also have been pintos and one or more of the so-called leopard horses which were introduced into Great Britain, Germany, and Denmark by the Spanish. The marking is very distinctive though it varies somewhat. In the United States horses with this marking are known as Appaloosas.

Whether the ancestors of our wild horses were strays or whether they were stolen by the Indians is not known. Some authorities insist that they were gifts, and that the invaders encouraged the native Indians to breed and raise horses. Other authorities question this, saying that the escaped horses lived as wild horses propagating in the wild regions, and were caught and tamed much later. Whatever the truth, in the Western plains there developed a distinctive type of wild horse, valued by the Indians as mounts in warfare and later by the settlers. From these wild mustangs our present day Western horse is descended, though it is doubtful if there are any of pure Mustang blood remaining.

Type and Conformation

The life of freedom which he enjoyed for so many generations left its stamp both physically and temperamentally on the Cow Pony. Since his first and fundamental instinct was that of survival, and since he had many wild enemies, the Western Horse became wary, intelligent, tough, strong, quick on his feet, and sturdy. He can keep fit on a sparse diet and can go without water for long periods. His bone is dense and strong, and his hoofs are not nearly as brittle as those of Thoroughbreds, which have been coddled in stables or run on soft turf. He is not a big horse, but is surprisingly fast, especially in starting, stopping, and turning.

Temperament and Intelligence

The Western Horse shows his superior intelligence in two ways. He readily learns his job, whether as cutting horse, roping horse, rodeo performer, parade horse, or trail horse. Once he understands what is expected of him he can be depended on to continue with little or no help from his master. For speed in starting and for handiness, the only other horse that is comparable is the Polo Pony, and, more times than not, he is of the same ancestry. However, partly due to his intelligence and often because of the way he is originally handled, the Western Horse can be very unreliable. Whereas the Arab for generations was considered a member of the family, the Western Horse prefers his independence and very often obeys simply out of fear. He must be roped when caught, because he has not been gentled and petted. He accepts what he has been taught, but under unknown conditions he will fight rather than trust his master.

Training

It is only natural that, with horses to be had for the catching, and with so many hundreds to be made into useful beasts in the shortest possible time, the cowboy took the quickest way. Mares bore their foals in the pasture. Except when they were rounded up for castration and branding, the foals knew no handling until they were three- or four-year-olds. To them, man was to be feared. To the cowboy, the young horses were animals that must be shown who was boss. So the method was to rope the horse, tie him down, slap on a saddle, get on and ride him to a standstill. He was encouraged to buck, and if he didn't buck by nature, he was raked with sharp spurs to make him do so. If he wanted to run, he was made to run until he couldn't take another step. In any event, the cowboy stayed aboard until the horse had discovered that no matter how he tried to escape, he must submit to this new master. Only when that was established, was he ready for any further training.

This method of breaking is still being used in some places. But good horses today are scarcer and much more valuable. Owners are finding that "rough" breaking the colts, starting at such a late age. is too costly. Many, treated this way, become outlaws, and horses as well as riders can be severely injured in the process. More modern breeders and owners are following the advice of the American Quarter Horse Association. This organization publishes a very good brochure, "Training Riding Horses," in which it explains, with clear text and good pictures, the opposite method of training, that of accustoming the young foal to being handled and taught to submit to his training, not through fear but because he trusts his master.

It is interesting to note that the Indians also used patience and gentleness in training their ponies, even though they usually caught them after they were full grown. Instead of roping and throwing the terrified animal, the Indian, after roping him, spent several hours teaching him that even though man was strange, he was not to be feared, and that no matter how terrifying his master's movements might be, the young horse would not be hurt so long as he stood quietly.

PHYSICAL STAMINA

The speed and stamina of Western Mustangs is best demonstrated by the use to which he was put during the short era of the Pony Express. Generally speaking, these horses worked in relays, going at the full gallop over every kind of terrain for a specified number of miles, usually under twenty. But there is one record which speaks of a Pony Express rider who for six months covered a hundred miles a night, for three successive nights each week, resting the other four. At the end of that period, which coincided with the discontinuance of the corps, he and his pony were both in good condition. These horses also proved their ability to stick to their training, with or without the direction of the rider. The mail was always strapped to the saddle, and in several instances, the riders were shot down by bandits, but the pony continued on to the next station, with the mail intact.

Usage Today and in the Future

The jeep is beginning to replace the horse for certain duties such as fence riding, but no vehicle will ever replace the Cutting Horse or the horse taught to keep a tight rope on a steer while the rider dismounts and ties up the animal. For this reason, as long as there are cattle ranches, there will be trained horses and cowboys to ride them. Of course the time may come, as it has in chicken farming and also in the dairy business, where it has been found more profitable to keep the animals strictly confined, feeding them on forage and grains rather than putting them out to pasture. Grass may now be grown economically in water with chemicals added. A small building, ten-by-twelve and eight feet high, containing a simple arrangement of trays, will grow five hundred pounds of oat grass every twenty-four hours. This is enough to provide green forage for about sixty milk cows and has been shown to increase their daily output of milk by one or two pounds over those being fed a balanced and nutritious diet but without the hydroponic grass. Even in grass-growing countries, many horse-breeding farms are putting in hydroponic units on the theory that the rich oat grass increases the fertility of the stallions and improves the condition of both mares and foals. Riding stables in parts of the country where the pasture season is very short or where land is too valuable to be used for pasturage are finding it economical to turn to the hydroponic units also, as supplementary feeding to take the place of part of the hay-and-grain ration. With the perpetual problem of water shortage in certain cattle areas, perhaps our beef animals will shortly find themselves standing in sheds and being fed silage, hay, and hydroponically grown grass from birth to butcher.

Rodeo and Horse Show Competition

Nevertheless, even though the above should come to pass, the highly trained Cutting and Roping Horse will find a place for himself in the rodeo horse show arenas and the art will never be lost.

These differ greatly from other horse shows. Rodeos started as informal contests on individual ranches. Later they were organized on a national and international scale. In Canada there is the Calgary Stampede, a tremendous affair that goes on for a week and attracts acts, exhibitions, and competitors from every part of North America. Similar events are held annually in the Far West, the Southwest, and even in New York's Madison Square Garden. Many of the entries are young men and women who spend all their time training themselves and their horses and competing in these contests. These events always include steer and calf roping, cutting, bronco riding, wild-horse riding, fancy roping, and steer riding. Most of the events are judged on time as well as correct execution. As these events become bigger and more popular, many more horses and riders are under training.

The Western horse show is controlled mainly by the National Cutting Horse Association and its affiliates and is a slightly more formal affair. The general setup resembles a horse show of any kind. Some of these shows are all Western, while in others there is a Western division. The rules for judging each event are carefully laid out, and the judges are skillful.

There are several types of classes in these shows. In breeding classes, the animal is shown in hand and is judged on quality, and conformation according to his type or bloodlines (Quarterhorse, Arabian, Palomino, Pinto, Appaloosa, etc). The Pleasure Horses are judged on manners, quality, and suitability as comfortable trail or saddle horses. In Parade Horses, the emphasis is on style, flash, gait, and equipment both of horse and rider. The final classification is for Stock Horses that have been trained for one of the following: working cowhorse, reining, roping, cutting, barrel racing, bending, or obstacle racing. Rules for these contests are very stringent. A definite course is laid out, and in most of them, each contestant enters alone and is judged on his speed, manners, ease of handling, flexibility, willingness, intelligence, etc. In Cutting contests, where the rider is asked to single out an animal and separate him from a herd, once the specified animal is indicated, the horse must do the whole thing by himself with no help from the rider—the latter being considered a passenger.

In the Working Cowhorse tests the horse is asked to start, stop, turn on his hindquarters, and sometimes to take a roping test. At one point he is required to drag for a given distance a sack which has been attached to the saddle horn by a rope. The horse must keep the rope taut while the rider dismounts and walks down its length to the sack.

Barrel racing is intended to test the horse's agility to turn at speed. The barrels are set in a triangle forty yards apart, except at the base where the distance is thirty-five yards. The competitor enters and gallops straight through the center to the apex barrel where he bends around and then follows the pattern of the triangle, circling each barrel. This is a popular competition with both men and women, and it is astounding to see the horses turning so sharply that they appear to be almost flat on their sides.

In the early days many of these contests were cruel, but today, with penalties for the horses' thrown back heads and open mouths, the cowboys must train their mounts to do everything on a light rein and without the use of cruelly long curb bits.

The race track is still another field in which the Stock Horse is becoming prominent. For many years the Quarterhorse has been popular for this sport, and the American Quarterhorse Association has done much to promote Quarterhorse racing. Today we find other breeds, such as Pintos, being organized into racing competitions. All of these activities insure the continuance of Stock Horse breeding, even when and if their original purpose as a working horse on a ranch has diminished.

Quarterhorse racing

Quarter Horse Journal

Quarterhorse

The term "Quarterhorse" does not derive, as one might suppose, from the strong muscular quarters usually so prominently displayed in photographs of this breed, but from the early days in Virginia when there were no tracks for flat racing and few highways with long straightaways where two cavaliers might challenge each other to a sprint. However, it was possible, on occasion, to find a suitable stretch of open road as much as a quarter of a mile in length. Horses that could get away to a fast start and go at full speed for this distance became popular and were termed Quarterhorses to designate the length of the race.

ORIGIN AND HISTORY

The foundation sire of the breed was an English Thoroughbred named Janus, brought to this country for breeding purposes and kept as a stud

A typical quarterhorse photograph — Leo Zero

Quarter Horse Journal

in Virginia from 1756 to 1780. He was a heavy-built animal, standing only fourteen-two with heavy, bulging muscles. He was raced over four-mile courses, but his get all showed a tremendous potentiality for the shorter contests. Every registered Quarterhorse today traces his descent back to Janus.

From Virginia the Quarterhorse went west with the pioneers. Like the Morgans, even after generations of cross breeding his type retained its original characteristics. Since his hardiness, speed, intelligence, and docility made him the ideal horse for all types of work in the settling of the West, it is no wonder that these characteristics have been cherished and, consequently, have improved rather than deteriorated.

TYPE AND CONFORMATION

It is the bulging type of muscle and the fact that he carries most of his weight on his forehand that enables the Quarterhorse to get off to a speedy start. For that very reason he tires quickly. In appearance he is very different from the Thoroughbred and from the Standardbred, both of which are bred for staying power. His legs are much shorter, and his muscles, especially those of his jaw, shoulder, thigh, and gaskin, are round rather than flat. Though a good hand shorter than the average Thoroughbred (few are taller than sixteen hands), he weighs about the same (an average of twelve hundred pounds). Temperamentally he has an even disposition, and since his skin is fairly thick, flies do not bother him. He can live off the land as do the Stock Horses.

USAGE TODAY

Today the Quarterhorse is valued not only for his performance on the ranch, in the horse show and rodeo arena and on the track, but also very highly in the stud, for he is used to improve the get of Range Horses both here and in South America and Mexico. Indeed, in the latter country purebred Quarterhorses are becoming very common in the *charro* activities.

SHOWING AND RACING

The American Quarterhorse Association (AQHA), whose purpose is to set up a registry for the breed, was formally established on March 15, 1940, at Fort Worth, Texas. With the interest and help of this organization the breed has prospered. As more and more people became owners, and the breed increased in number, it became desirable to devise tests and an orderly system of awarding special honors to outstanding horses. Thus contests in cutting, reining, roping, barrel racing, working cowhorse, Western pleasure, and Western riding, as well as halter classes, were organized under specific rules of performance and judging. Records of winners at all approved shows were kept and the awards of Register of Merit and AQHA were given each year to the top horses in each division.

The American Quarterhorse Association also makes and enforces rules for recognized Quarterhorse racing. These races are of different lengths, up to but not exceeding 440 yards. The world record as of 1962 is as follows: 220 yards, 12:1 seconds; 259 yards, 13:4 seconds; 300 yards, 15:5; 330 yards, 16:9; 350 yards, 17:5; 400 yards, 19:9; and 440 yards, 21:7.

The AQHA is an active, forward-looking organization, with beautiful modern headquarters in Amarillo, Texas. It works with the state and county agricultural agents. In many states its Extension Service has specially designed manuals for use of the 4-H Club members, as well as a number of interesting pamphlets pertaining to the breeding, feeding, training, riding, and care of the Quarterhorse.

Cross Breeds

With Quarterhorse as the favored blood, different ranchers have introduced other bloodlines into their range horses, always with the idea of improving them for whatever specific purpose they are needed. Some, desiring to produce good half-bred Hunters, are using Thoroughbred stallions on Quarterhorse mares. The cross produces a high-quality Hunter that is much in demand in the East. This cross was also very popular for the production of cavalry mounts before the latter's breeding program was discontinued. Arabian blood has been found to be advantageous, especially for the breeding of a flashy type of horse used for parade work, and to improve the lighter-weight horses used for Polo Ponies. Many horses of mixed bloodlines are shipped all over North and South America every year, to be used as pleasure horses, hacks, children's mounts, etc., under English tack, as well as being trained to do the type of work for which they were originally bred.

I myself have had many of these Western-bred horses of indeterminate breeding in my stable. I have found them to have more individual personalities than any other breed. Two outstanding ones come to mind: Bobolink was a former Cavalry horse, probably Thoroughbred on range, with a little Quarterhorse somewhere along the line. He was an excellent Hunter and Jumper and very gentle with children. Like most of his kind, however, he had certain likes and dislikes. He always kept a good distance behind another horse when working in the school, and his idea of a good distance increased as he got older; he would not tolerate a whip. No one in the cavalry had been permitted to carry such an object, and he failed to see why a brash beginner should do so. He would allow the rider to take one from a bystander, but if it were used ever so lightly on any part of his body, up would go Bobolink's big haunches to send the luckless beginner flying through the air. Of course a good rider was not so treated, and in such a case Bobolink simply got sulkier and sulkier.

Spurs, however, were in a different category. Spurs were the ordinary equipment even of the recruit, and Bobolink had been taught to put up with them. Consequently, many parents were often horrified to see me, tired of shouting at Bobolink and waving my hat at him from behind when he refused to keep up his distance, take off my short but rowelled spurs and put them on the heels of the six-year-old just having his third or fourth lesson.

Bobolink was about seven when we bought him from a dealer. He was never lame a day and had no respiratory or eye troubles until he was well over twenty and was kicked in the pasture by a newly acquired gelding. Though his leg was not broken, the tendons were badly damaged and the nerve was affected. He was in great pain and there was little likelihood of a complete recovery. At the end of a week the poor fellow had to be put away, but he will always live in my heart.

Bonny, mentioned earlier in the discussion of Half-breds and Thoroughbreds, had one of the strongest characters of all my horses. She came in from the West in a carload of horses, and we bought her after she had had only a little training in the Hackamore and before she had been made afraid by being ridden in a severe bit.

Bonny was fourteen-one, stocky, with a well set-on head. She had a style that invariably caught the judge's eye, and she adored any kind of competition or show. She very quickly learned the show routine, knowing, for example that "Reverse and canter" would follow a period at the canter in one direction, and that in turn would be followed by "Walk, please" and then "line up." As soon as the "Walk, please" was given, Bonny often turned and lined up immediately. Riders who did not know this little trick sometimes found themselves rather disconcerted, even to the extent of picking them-

Bonny *over a jump*.

selves up off the ground, for when Bonny turned, her Cow Pony blood exerted itself and she turned very abruptly.

Bonny did not like anyone treading on her heels, and for this reason we usually put Bobolink behind her in the line, knowing that he would not get too close. Nor, as explained earlier, did she like spotted horses or ponies. She took the greatest pleasure in disciplining any animal that crowded her, letting fly at once, especially at the spotted ones. The instructor with a class of beginners had to be alert to forestall any such action, for when Bonny let fly it was with both heels raised high, and there was always the danger that the unfortunate rider of the other pony would be the recipient.

But in the show ring all this disappeared. I remember many years ago when my youngest daughter, then about six, was to ride Bonny in a local show. In those days the caliber of riders in novice classes, especially in those for children under twelve, was extremely low compared with what we see today. Gincy had done very little cantering even in class, and I did not expect that would be required in this show. The judges thought differently, though, and after watching the group of twenty or more youngsters at the walk and trot, they asked for a canter.

"Now, we'll have trouble," I thought, for the other children in the group were even more inexperienced than my daughter. No sooner was the command "Canter, please" given than there was a melee of galloping, out-of-hand ponies charging into one another (including into Bonny) or stopping short and refusing to budge. Furthermore, many of these were pintos. But, as I might have known, Bonny's desire to win a blue ribbon surmounted her natural inclination to discipline the other animals. With the reins hanging loose —for Gincy had been told to leave everything to her horse and just concentrate on staying in the saddle—the little mare cantered slowly around, weaving herself in and out, avoiding the balkers and paying no attention when one crashed into her. Certainly if ever a horse deserved that blue, she did. She came out of the ring, ears pricked, the blue hanging on her headstall and, once out of sight of the judges, let fly at once at an unsuspecting, out-of-control piebald that had dared to come within the specified four-foot distance. This happened as they were riding across the field towards where I was standing, waiting to congratulate Gincy and praise Bonny for her forebearance.

Bonny was also very opinionated about certain other things. For example in the stable she stood for a number of years in the first standing stall in a row. This stall she liked, and there was no reason why she couldn't have continued to have it, until the time came when she was about to become a mother. None of us thought that a standing stall only four by eight was a suitable foaling stall, so Bonny was promoted to the grandeur of a box stall. Did she approve of the promotion? Not at all! She would have none of the box stall and always found a way either to break out of it or to break away when she was being led toward it from the pasture. Then she would force her way into the line of standing stalls and kick or bite the temporary resident of her former stall until the latter either made his way out or was rescued.

We stood this for a week and then, since the weather was mild, decided to leave Bonny out day and night, bringing her in for feeding only, at which time we let her be in her own stall. This worked very well. Gincy, now about eleven, was doing the feeding that winter. One day she left for school, saying that Bonny was eating her oats and that she had put a pile of hay in the paddock for her. Ten minutes later I went out to see how everything was. There was Bonny standing up eating away, and on the cold cement floor behind her lay Meadow Lark! Inasmuch as it was her first colt, the mare hadn't even realized what was happening and had no idea that she had produced a fine son who was to become one of the best, if not the best, colt we have ever raised!

Color Classification

APPALOOSA

There are three types of horses which may be registered according to a color classification. These are the Appaloosa, the Palomino, and the Pinto. The Appaloosa's pattern, of small oval or round spots of black or chocolate on a white background, has been common in certain breeds of horses for many years. At least one of these, or a mare or stallion with this coloring in antecedents, must have come over with one of the importations of Spanish horses introduced by the conquistadores, for many appeared among the Mustangs of the West. The Indians particularly valued these horses, contending that they were hardier than horses of other colors. Many owners of Appaloosas today are in agreement with this theory, and a fine specimen of the "raindrop" or Appaloosa brings a high price.

One curious thing about this marking is that there is a slight difference in the texture of the white and dark areas so that the spots may be felt as well as seen. Not all Appaloosas are marked exactly alike; some have spots more or less evenly distributed over the entire body which is white while in others

Mischel's Columbia Studio

The Appaloosa stallion, Sass Thomas, *wins the Idaho State Open Barrel Racing Championship.*

the forehand is mottled and more or less dark without distinguishing spots, while the hindquarters are white with distinct spots. In most there is tendency for more visible white around the iris of the eye and longitudinal stripes of white on the hoofs. Appaloosas are used in performance contests in shows and rodeos where no special breed or type is specified, as well as in halter and performance classes limited to their own kind.

PALOMINO

Everyone today is familiar with the striking golden horses with silver manes and tails known as Palominos. This again is a breed where registry depends not on ancestry but on color. To be registered in the Palomino Horse Registry, the entry must be not more than three shades lighter or darker than a newly minted gold coin. The mane and tail must be white (known as flaxen) with not more than 15 per cent of chestnut or dark hairs in it. White markings on face and lower legs are permitted and very common, but there must be no white on the body. The skin and eyes must be dark. The Palomino Association is endeavoring to establish foundation sires which

Palomino parade horse, in full trappings

Jean A. Whitesell

Palomino parade horse

Ernie Belanger

will pass on the true color from generation to generation, but at the moment two Palominos bred together are less apt to produce a true golden foal than is the cross of one Palomino parent and one golden chestnut.

As might be supposed, the Palominos make especially spectacular Parade Horses as well as Western Saddle Hacks. Of course they vary tremendously in type, since the primary foundation strain may be Arabian, Quarterhorse, or a mixture. Palomino Saddlebreds are not unknown, though rare. Palomino ponies are becoming more and more popular, and we find both American Shetlands and Welsh with this coloring, as well as the mixed breeds which often get their coloring from Arabian ancestry. One of the most endearing horses I have ever seen was a tremendous Palomino draft stallion. He was standing in a corner stall of a rather rattletrap barn in the Post Road where I stopped one day to look at some young stock. The owner brough him out for me to see. He had a beautiful delicate head, with a mane and tail like dandelion down. The tail was especially noticeable, for it trailed on the ground behind him as he walked, leaving a little track in the dust. He had the disposition of an angel and delightful gaits. When I looked at his lovely broad back and big haunches (for he was built exactly like the white horses used in circuses for bareback trick riders) and saw him cantering gently around on a longe, I longed to buy him, for he would have made an ideal horse for teaching beginners to sit and canter. Furthermore I could have mounted at least four on him at once!

Pinto

The Pinto Horse Association is the most recently established, having been formed in 1956. Its address is Box 155, R.F.D. 1, Ellington, Connecuticut, and its president is Mr. Leo W. Carrier.

The word "Pinto" is Spanish, meaning "painted" or "colored." For many years horses with large spots on a solid background were known as "piebald" (black on white or white on black) or "skewbalds" (white with spots of any color other than black). The Association chose to call itself the Pinto Horse Association, since this covered horses of both descriptions. It has further classified its members as those of "Overo" markings and those with "Tobiano" markings. The Overo (in the registration such horses retain the letter *O* in their number) is described as follows: "A colored horse, roan dun, sorrel, bay, brown, or black with white extending upward and irregular

Ray M. Watson

A Mare Pinto Class in Springdale, Arkansas, showing both Tobiano and Overo Markings

in pattern. Mane and tail dark or mixed, head usually white or bald (dark with white face). Legs usually have a combination of white and solid color."

The Tobiano (*T*) shows a "clearly marked pattern with white as a base and another color usually divided about half and half throughout the coat. Mane and tail are the color of the region from which they stem. Legs are usually white; head dark or combined with markings such as star, stripe, snip, or blaze."

Origin and History: In tracing the history of the colored horse, Carl E. Raswan points out that this coloring was one which developed in primeval times in areas where there were sharply contrasting lights and shadows, and served the same purpose as the stripes of the zebras and the spots of the giraffes, namely that of camouflage. He believes also that the American Indians, realizing this, prized them as war ponies.

Pintos were found to be common in Tibet and in the Himalayas. Crossing with Mongolian ponies coarsened the type, but later selective breeding with

Arabian stock improved it. There is a great variety of animal type, since this is a color classification, rather than a type or breed, and has bloodlines of many kinds in its background. Probably the best known is the sturdy, short-coupled, workmanlike animal used as a performance horse and stock horse. Many of these are exceedingly handsome animals, especially when the head is not too coarse. There is also a more lightly built type, somewhat on the Arabian conformation, and a longer, slender type, with the legs of a racer.

Some Pintos have won great fame as jumpers on the International Show teams. Probably the most famous Pinto in fiction is The Pie of *National Velvet*, who was ridden to victory in the Grand National by the butcher's daughter of that name.

Bobby Burke up on Mrs. Winston Guest's pinto Harlequin

Allen, Middleburg, Va.

Rodeos and Shows for Horses of Different Color Classifications

The classes in rodeos and shows in the West include horses classified as to color and are seldom limited to those of one color. Occasionally, however, one finds classes in the working divisions limited to horses of special color classifications (Palomino, Appaloosa, or Pinto). No doubt this tendency will increase as numbers of the various breeds become larger, and where the interest warrants it, there will be shows limited exclusively to classes for each of the above types of horses.

CHAPTER VI

Pony Division

Many laymen do not understand the distinction between the term "horse" as opposed to the term "pony." To clarify this, let us say that there are certain breeds of animals descended from purebred stock whose outstanding characteristic is their small size. These have always been known as "ponies." The most common of such breeds found today in the United States are the Shetland, Welsh, and Hackney ponies.

There are also numerous animals of mixed breeds or indeterminent bloodlines that are small. Some of these may have no purebred pony bloodlines at all. Yet, because they are small—fourteen hands two inches (fifty-eight inches) is the dividing line—these too are classified as "ponies."

In addition, there are two types of horses which, though usually over the fourteen-two limit, are still called "ponies." The first of these is the Stock Horse, often called a Cowpony. The second is the animal used in polo, always known as a Polo Pony. One should remember, in connection with the usage of the term "pony" for an animal that today is most certainly a horse and often large, that the little Mustang was seldom over fourteen-two, and the first mounts used by the English for polo in India were little Mongolian ponies thirteen hands two inches and under.

On the other side of the picture there are several breeds of horses, notably the Arabian and the Quarterhorses, which often include many animals well under fourteen-two. These are always called "horses." Yet in open competition for ponies, such as Pony Jumpers, Pony Hunters, Equitation Ponies, etc., these so-called horses are eligible to compete if they are within the specified size limits.

To sum this up, for showing and for general terminology, all animals regardless of bloodlines are correctly referred to as "ponies" if they do not stand higher than fourteen hands two inches at the withers.

Iceland ponies imported to Hamburg, Germany by Mrs. Ursula Schaum-burg (left.)

ORIGIN AND HISTORY

The pony is of northern stock. His primeval ancestors roamed the tundras of the Far North. The Tarpan was a primitive North European horse indigenous to southern Russia, Poland, and Hungary. His ancestors were the prehistoric horses found in America that moved south, crossing into Europe with the Ice Age. This pony was gray and of a light build, having some Arabian in his bloodlines. Although the Tarpan is extinct, similar animals are being produced today by Professor Lutz Heck of Berlin.

The yellow wild horse of the northern steppes of Mongolia and Asia is known as the Przevalski. It was so named in honor of Colonel N. M. Przevalski, who obtained the skin and skull of one of these animals. This is also the

Wide World Photo

Three miniature Shetland ponies in Sussex, England, the smallest of which is only 17¼ inches high and weighs about 12 pounds.

"wild horse" depicted on the walls and ceilings of caves in France and Spain. This horse survives today. He is a pony in size also.

In 1902 an expedition to the Gobi Desert captured some immature animals (it was found impossible to capture the adults) and these have been carefully studied. Herds move through the Mongolian steppes and deserts, and, though too wild to be trained, they mix and breed with the Mongolian Ponies.

Physical Characteristics of the Pony

The primeval pony developed a thick skin and very heavy coat because of the intense cold. His head was large and of the "ram" or "Roman" shape as opposed to the delicate "dish" profile of the Arabian. This was due to the need of modifying the temperature of the air before it passed directly into the lungs. To insure this, the nostrils were narrow and did not flare open when the horse panted, and the nasal passages were very large.

The teeth of the primeval pony and of the Mongolian and Icelandic ponies today have extraordinarily long roots. Much of the forage they eat is not grass but sticks, bark, and twigs. This means that the surfaces of the teeth are worn away very quickly and the teeth must have long roots to replace them. The tail of the true pony is kept tucked into the buttocks instead of being high set as in the desert horse. This again is due to the need to conserve warmth. The walls of hoofs are much less brittle than those of horses, especially the Arabian and Thoroughbreds; for the hardy wild ponies roamed in rocky country rather than in pasture land or sandy desert.

Through the introduction of Arabian and other bloodlines, the popular pony of today is a very different creature from his ancestor. In Europe, especially in certain parts of Scandinavia and in Iceland, as well as in Asia, this is not true. The Icelandic Pony, for example, is much nearer to the original pony type and is hardier than some of the more modern breeds.

Temperament and Intelligence

The physical characteristics of the primeval horses have contributed a great deal to the modern pony's character. Because his skin was and is today thicker than that of the "hot-blooded" horse, he is less sensitive than the latter and does not react as quickly. On the other hand, neither does he become hysterical so easily as the more sensitive horse. He is not so uncomfortable under the ignorant hands and legs of the tyro and so will put up with much more mistreatment without trying to take revenge either on his rider or on another pony.

In the northern climates forage was scarce. It was necessary for the pony to spend most of his life on the move. He never had the domestic training of the Arabian horse nor was he kept in herds in grassy lowlands. This may account in part for the urge of the pony to wander, for it is certain that he is not "stable bound" as is the average horse. He will be content in his own pasture for only a short time, no matter how good the grass is. Then he wants to move on into the neighbor's lot.

The pony is crafty. Not only does he use every kind of ingenuity in breaking out of field, paddock, or stable, but he also knows exactly what he can get away with. If the rider is ignorant and the pony not too well trained, the latter will soon become master.

The pony's temperament is affected in great part by diet. Grain is very stimulating to an animal whose ancestors lived on roots and twigs for a large part of the year. A pony that, grass-fed, is amiable and willing may turn into a kicking, biting, unmanageable beast if kept stabled, grained, and underexercised.

Uses

For many years ponies were considered highly unsuitable as mounts for young children. This was chiefly because their owners did not understand how to train or care for them. Ponies as such are not native to this country. Shetland, Welsh, and Moor ponies are all foreigners. Yet, in England, these same ponies were used consistently and successfully by children of all ages both in harness and the hunt field and for general purposes. A few American riding instructors and some experienced parents discovered that the well-trained pony was an ideal companion and mount for the young child. Today our beliefs have been vindicated and the Pet and Hunting Pony has never been more popular. For the timid little beginner there are the tiny "miniatures" of nine hands or so. For the child of ten or twelve who is experienced, the show ring has classes for larger, more spirited animals. Let us now examine the various types and breeds to be found at the dealers and on the breeding farms.

Shetland

The original Shetlands came from the Shetland Isles and were principally used for drawing the coal carts in the mines. They were short, heavy-set, and strong, with big necks and rather coarse heads. Most were under forty-two inches and many as small as thirty-eight. Except in the governess cart they were not suitable for the young child, for their backs were too broad

Prize-winning Shetland ponies in London. Notice how stocky they are compared to the American Shetland.

and flat and their necks too thick. However, when these animals were imported and especially with the introduction of Arabian blood, the type changed. The American Shetland (Pet Pony) has lost the coarse neck and the mutton shoulders. He is built much more like the Welsh.

It was this type of Shetland that I was able to buy in Virginia when my own children were small. At that time there was a breeding farm with three or four hundred ponies near Front Royal. Colonel Elliot, who owned the farm, had a good system of training and marketing his stock. The mares and foals roamed the fields and hills until the latter were weaned at the age of six months. At that time they were separated. The mares were left out in the far pasture, while the foals were kept in nearby fields and paddocks where they were handled every day, halter broken, taught to stand still when groomed and not to fear man. They were then turned back out together with their mothers again.

As yearlings they were once more rounded up. Now their serious work began. They were longed and then driven regularly by expert trainers. As two-year-olds they were ridden, but again only by young people who know their jobs. From about the age of two and a half to three, depending on how their education was progressing, Colonel Elliot listed them in his catalogue as being available to buyers. He was always very meticulous in stating their exact dispositions (alert, lively, very gentle, sluggish, etc.), their degree of training, and for what type of rider they were suitable. His catalogue contained the names and descriptions of some three hundred ponies of all kinds. All were registered Shetlands but they varied greatly in size and type. Over the years we bought more than twelve ponies from Colonel Elliot and they always lived up to their description. Several times I simply wrote the colonel, told him the age, experience, and temperament of the child for whom I was buying the pony, and he invariably picked out a suitable one. My own ponies, Jess and Shoebutton, both came from the Colonel's Belle Meade Farm. Shoey lived to be thirty and Jess about as long, and I would never exchange the training that they gave my children for any other type of activity whatsoever.

There are still pony farms which specialize in these general, all-purpose Shetlands. There are also pony farms which raise useful Pet Ponies or animals destined for the show ring. Many of these are the really miniature type. I stopped off several years ago to visit such a breeding farm when I was coming back from a lecture tour. We were in the neighborhood of

Shoebutton, *a hunting or pet pony type of American Shetland stock*

Roanoke, Virginia, when we saw a sign PONIES FOR SALE outside a rather ramshackle-looking barn. It was not a very good day to look at ponies, being drizzly and gray, but we went in anyway, expecting to be shown perhaps a dozen animals. To our surprise this barn housed several hundred of the miniature type and I have seldom seen any gentler or more appealing animals. Eight little stallions stood in a row tethered to a picket line. None was over thirty-six inches high at the withers and many were under. They looked like little fairy horses; their tails dragged on the ground, and their manes were so soft and silky and full that often only the very tips of the ears were visible. There were no separating partitions but the eight little stallions kept to their assigned spaces without any bickering.

The brood mares were turned out, but there were two big areas of colts, one for weanlings and the other for yearlings. Here tiny little creatures roamed together, friendly and gentle, coming up to have their noses rubbed. I longed to take home at least six and train a driving team to pull a miniature coach. Unfortunately, though their size makes them enchanting, these very small ponies are really only proportioned for the child under five or six. They are very strong, however, and do make excellent driving ponies.

American Shetland, Harness Type

Only in the last decade or two has the registered American Shetland changed from being an all-purpose pony to what amounts to a miniature Hackney with all of the latter's fire, flash, and fineness. This has been accomplished through the introduction of Hackney bloodlines, training, and shoeing. These little high-steppers with their long hoofs are suitable for showing only. Contrary to the Hackneys, they wear their tails long and flowing. They are judged by the same standards as are the other Fine Harness breeds. The interest in these ponies has become so great in certain parts of the country that the prices have soared to unbelievable heights: Six or seven thousand dollars for a filly with no show record, for example. This is a far higher price than is paid for registered animals of other breeds. So high have the prices become that the only buyers are other breeders and show stables. Eventually there should be a saturation point at which time the fad will probably lapse and the prices will come down. Then there may be a chance for the return of the Harness Shetland as we used to know him, namely an attractive, small but not tiny pony, suitable for a child.

American Shetland, harness type, shown in the "Fancy Turnout" Class where costumes and vehicle count 60 per cent.

Welsh Mountain Pony

One of the most popular breeds of pony, and rightly so, is the Mountain Welsh breed. These ponies are slightly larger than the smallest of the Shetlands, and more finely built. Their heads are often Arabian in type. They usually have very good dispositions although they are sometimes inclined to be a little more nervous than the phlegmatic Shetlands. They have tremendous aptitude in jumping and make excellent Hunting Ponies.

Native to the mountains of Wales, these ponies, as well as the Welsh Cob and the ordinary Welsh, are among the oldest of breeds. Welsh mares, crossed with Arabian and Thoroughbred blood, were the founders of many lines of Polo Pony stock. They are tremendously strong, even though they lack the apparent sturdiness of the Shetlands. Like the latter, they were

A Welsh pony

used in the coal mines, but of late years they have been so valuable as children's mounts that they have been rescued from the plebeian fate.

A Welsh pony may be any color other than spotted. The most popular color has always been gray. These ponies are invariably among the winners in all horse show classes for ponies under saddle. Mrs. Ellie Wood Keith was one of the earliest promoters of the Welsh pony and as far back as the nineteen twenties had several imported stallions and mares.

Last summer we had the good fortune to be loaned a registered Welsh Mountain Pony who had a foal at heel. I have never met a more charming or more reliable animal. She was only four years old herself and had had very little training, but she learned readily both to ride and drive. Furthermore, she was a perfect lady when it came to stable and field manners. She would stand for hours while my daughter's three-and-a-half-year-old twins scrubbed away with brush and curry comb and tried to climb up her legs. Then, with an older but very inexperienced rider, she would trot along the roads or canter gaily over the fields. Her little foal had the same beautiful disposition and was allowed to run loose on the lawn. He quickly learned the value of walking out onto the edge of the road when he saw a car approaching and looking so longingly at it that the driver invariably stopped to talk to him and sometimes provided him with a tidbit. Unlike most young colts being fed out of the hand, this one never seemed to pick up the habit of nipping.

The mare, the foal, and a Shetland were pastured a little away from the house in good weather. One night in the late fall a northeast storm came up in the middle of the night. There were trees for shelter but the rain was a driving one, and when I went to get the ponies in the next morning they were soaking wet. The mare and the Shetland gelding came up quietly as usual, glad to be taken in out of the storm, but accepting the latter as something to be expected. Not so Candy, the foal. He was now about five months old and this was his first experience with a seashore gale. He reasoned that the whole thing was my fault, and before I had time to get the halters on the other ponies in order to lead them home, he backed his little rump up to me and kicked as hard as he could, just to express his resentment! This was the first time anyone had ever seen him lift a heel from the ground either in anger or play, but he was really angry. I had a hard time collecting the older ponies out of the pasture and down the road, for every few minutes Candy would come back to tell me again how annoyed he was. Usually he followed quietly enough at their heels as I led the others down the public road, but not today. He galloped ahead, he stopped and caprioled several times, dove again at me and bucked and caprioled some more. Never have I seen a member of the equine race express himself to a human so deliberately and so successfully!

Moor Ponies

There are a number of ponies indigenous to the broad moors of England. The Dartmoor and the Exmoor are probably the most popular, although there are not many of them in this country. These ponies are slightly larger than the Welsh and Shetlands. They have sturdy bodies on clean legs, and their dispositions are excellent. Most run between thirteen and fourteen hands in height and can be any weight. In the United States they are ridden only by children, but in Europe and England they are popular

Wild ponies from Assateague Island are driven across Assateague Channel to Chincoteague in the annual pony-penning.

as trail ponies for adults as well. The Dartmoor Ponies have survived in a rugged type of country where provender is scarce. The Exmoor Ponies come from a somewhat warmer climate, and are supposed to be direct descendants of the original British Wild Horse. Both types are solid colors, and the mealy nose of the Exmoor is one of its distinguishing features.

I have not had many purebred Moor Ponies, but a few years ago a beautiful Exmoor specimen came into the stable. He has proved one of the best ponies we have ever had, being thoroughly reliable under beginners, yet good enough to win the shows, both on the flat and over jumps. I was told that he gave a great deal of trouble in breaking, which is supposed to be one of the characteristics of these ponies, but he has absolutely no vices now. The fact that these ponies are large and sturdy and so can be broken to adults is probably why, even though they are wild at first, they end up being thoroughly reliable and well mannered.

Chincoteague Ponies

The Chincoteague Ponies, natives of a small island called Assateague off the coast of Virginia, are purported to be the descendants of some Moorish Ponies which swam ashore from a shipwreck that had occurred near there. Once a year the yearlings are rounded up, separated from the herd, and swum across to the island of Chincoteague where they are auctioned off. I have never had any personal contact with a purebred Chincoteague. They are said to be sturdy but very difficult to train. Once properly broken, however, they make good children's mounts.

Canyon Pony

This is a freakish type of dwarf horse, rather than a breed of pony. Many years ago, stray Mustangs found themselves trapped in one or more of the very deep canyons of the West. Every few decades a very small breed of horse is discovered there, stunted by the inbreeding and by the lack of forage. Some of these little horses (for they are built like horses and have no pony characteristics) are smaller than a good-sized dog and are more useful as exhibitiion animals than anything else.

Hackney Pony

The history of the Hackney Horse and Pony as a breed is covered in a later section in this book. The Hackney Harness Pony is one of the most popular of show breeds. It holds the same place in the harness pony picture as does the American Saddle Horse in his division. We have Roadsters, Western Hunter Hacks, etc., all shown under the saddle, but unquestionably the horse that catches the eye and stirs the enthusiasm is the American Saddler with his peacock airs, his flash, and his fire. The same is true of the Hackney Pony. His action is phenomenal; his knees coming almost to his chest, he seems like a bundle of nerves so sensitive that only the fine hands of an expert horseman can hope to communicate successfully with him through the reins.

In large show classes, Hackneys are often divided into groupings of small, medium, and large. The correlating height requirements are: under twelve:two hands, twelve:two and under thirteen:one, thirteen:one and not over fourteen:two. Classes may be limited further to stallions, mares, or

Hackney bay mare, 12:3 hands, is shown in a ladies' class.

geldings, shown singly, in pairs, or in tandem. Four-in-hands are usually matched in color and shown to a park drag, or they may be shown in a road coach and need not be matched in color.

In classes in which ladies are to drive emphasis is put on manners. In all classes quality, manners, performance, and soundness are considered.

Hard roads and motor traffic have taken the Hackney Pony off the roads and relegated him to the show ring. He is too nervous, and his gaits are too rough to make him a suitable children's Hack. But an admixture of his blood, especially when the other parent is a more phlegmatic breed such as Shetland, improves the sensitivity, speed, and jumping ability of the progeny.

One of the most outstanding ponies we had was a little bay named Shooting Star. I am not absolutely certain of her ancestry but she unquestionably had a good deal of Hackney blood and probably either Shetland or Welsh Mountain. As may be guessed from her name, she really soared through the air and, though only twelve hands, could clear three feet with ease. She was not a beginners' mount, having the thin skin of her Hackney ancestry, but was thoroughly reliable under the more sensitive rider. One of my sons took a fancy to her when he was about eleven years old. Up until then his favorite mount had been the little Shetland stallion, Shoebutton, who was only forty-two inches in height. But Toby's legs had finally gotten too long, and with regret he had to pick something else. Shooting Star was his choice. Toby was not a conventional horseman. To him a mount was not just a means of conveyance nor was he interested in preparing a horse for the show ring. He never used a saddle and often had no bridle either. When he rode, his horse became an extension of his own body and mind and had to learn to be completely responsive to whatever his whim might be. Games were his great love, and many a time have I seen him come galloping across the field on Star, bareback, no bridle, pursued by an older boy or girl on a larger animal. The game was a wild form of hide and go seek, with the "den" being the end of the stable. At a dead run Toby and Shooting Star would go through a gap in the stone wall, make a sharp left turn and then, still at the gallop, she would go up the runway which led to the stalls. As she went through the narrow door he would reach above, grasp the lintel of the door and swing off her back while she clattered down the runway to her stall.

He had been riding her only a short time when he had taught her to imitate a rocking horse. Collecting her first, he would signal and she would do a little levade, followed immediately by planting her front feet and kicking out behind. This she would repeat, going from forehand to hindquarters again and again without moving forward. He also used to drive her over the snow hitched to a sled, and he thought nothing of taking her around the two-foot-six pony jumps of the outside course.

Shooting Star's jumping ability was so outstanding that we bred her to the little Thoroughbred stallion, Meadow Whisk, and got a beautiful colt whom we called Meadow Moonshine, or Mooney for short. Although both sire and dam were bays, Mooney was a golden chestnut. He was thirteen-two when grown and looked exactly like a Thoroughbred Hunter seen through the wrong end of an opera glass.

From the time he was weaned, Mooney was one of the most endearing yet one of the most aggravating of animals. He learned tricks readily and adored showing off. He would count indefinitely and the signal used to stop him was so imperceptible that audiences were always puzzled when he did

Life magazine

Meadow Moonshine *plays seesaw.*

the most complicated mathematical problems with no difficulty. We also taught him to ride a seesaw and a rocking horse stand, which he loved.

He inherited both his mother's and his father's propensity for jumping. We do not jump our colts until they are at least three years old—and then only over low jumps for the first year. Mooney was one of those rare animals that adore jumping from the very beginning and never have to be schooled. When he was about three and a half, after only a few months of schooling, we allowed a boy to take him into a children's knock-down-and-out class where the jumps started at two feet six inches. It was a very small, unrecognized show at which Mooney first appeared in public over jumps, and it never occurred to any of us that the jumps would go much above three feet. But there was one competitor, a child on a retired open jumper, whose mount was an old hand. After the first two rounds, with the jumps standing at three feet and three inches, the field was reduced to Mooney and this horse. Nothing could stop the bold little pony. The boy had never gone higher than three-six, but he was game and as the jumps got higher he simply held on to the mane and left it all to the pony. At four feet and six inches the old horse finally knocked down the last bar and Mooney won with a clean round.

The next day he was lame. We spent three years trying to find out where the weakness lay. The veterinarians whom we called blistered, poulticed, wet-bandaged, and rubbed every part of his leg from the shoulder down, with no results. There was no specific swelling or sore spot. They recommended rest in a box stall. This seemed to do no good, so they suggested turning him into a small paddock for exercise. The paddock had a five-foot sheep-hurdle fence around it. Mooney, standing on three legs, took a look at the fence and then at the green fields. He took a few hobbling steps and, from a halt, soared through the air over the fence and departed at a gallop. Naturally when caught, he was even lamer! One summer we were sending some horses to Vermont to be prepared for competition in the Vermont Hundred Mile Ride. We sent Mooney along to be turned out in the Vermont hills and pastures for six months, in hopes that nature and the necessity of wandering up and down the hills would strengthen whatever muscles and ligaments were affected. At the end of the time Mooney returned, not so lame as when he left, but I noticed that after only a little work he was prone to go short again. We tried every type shoeing and we used rubber pads without notable success.

He was too much pony for a beginner, and of course we didn't dare jump him, so he hardly earned his keep. However, we kept him until he was twelve years old. Then a neighboring child who was a good little rider asked if she might take him to keep for trail riding. She lived in Greenwich, Connecticut, and had a hunter but badly wanted a pony as a pet. So Mooney left us and went to Greenwich, and now comes the remarkable part of the story. When he arrived there, his lameness completely disappeared. At the end of a year the child called and said that she had been galloping over the trails and, while hopping a log or a low stone wall, was it all right to jump him? I told her to go slowly and watch him carefully. Mooney is now seventeen. The last word I got was that he was being shown consistently in children's Hunter and Jumper classes, that he was winning regularly, and that he was still sound.

The answer? I just don't know. Sometimes I have thought that Mooney liked all the petting and care and lack of work that lameness brought him. He probably hated being ridden by a variety of riders and preferred jumping and doing tricks to everything else; but I hate to admit that a pony of my own breeding and raising could fool me over a period of nine long years!

CHAPTER VII

Miscellany

Hackney Horse

ORIGIN

The term "Hackney" comes from an early French word *hacquenee*, which in turn is derived from the Latin *equus*, meaning "horse." A still earlier term, "Nag," is from the Anglo-Saxon *hnegan*, meaning "to neigh," but by the early thirteen hundreds Hackney, meaning a general utility horse whose natural gait was the trot, had come into use. In these early days horses were classified by use as War Horses (generally gallopers), Hunting and Race Horses (also gallopers), Pacers and Amblers, Saddlers and Trotting Horses, which were popular as Saddlers for squires and yeomen as well as being used later in light cavalry. There was also the common draft animal used for plowing.

When the Romans invaded Britain, they found good horses and no doubt did what they could to improve the native stock by importations and selective breeding. The Danes and Norsemen imported horses which had special talents of their own, including the will to trot. These resulted in the so-called Norfolk Trotter, a road horse found in Norfolk and Yorkshire which was outstanding for its sturdiness, trotting ability, and solid conformation.

A Hackney horse pulls a buggy.

Carl Klein Photo

As early as 1495 efforts were being made through the English legislature to preserve and improve the breed of Road Horses. No one could deport any horses, mares, geldings, colts or stallions without special permission from the king, and as time went on, further acts were passed increasing the fines for disobeying the law. Also introduced was the penalty of being required to obtain and maintain a Trotting Horse as punishment for certain other offenses.

Trotting Horses of native stock were valued for their stamina as well as for their speed, being required to stand up under the test of forty, fifty, or even sixty miles a day, carrying a fully equipped cavalryman. They were valued as coach horses and the fast coaches were called Hackney Coaches to distinguish them from the heavier coaches pulled by horses of the heavier but slower type.

The sportsman who hunted regularly rode to the meet on a Hackney where his servant met him with his Hunter. At this time tandem driving came into favor. The Hunter was hitched as leader where he did no work, and the Hackney was between the shafts; thus the lover of the sport could conduct both horses to the covert site without tiring his Hunter, and then turn the Hackney and the dog cart over to his groom.

Since so much emphasis was put on speed, it is doubtful if these early horses or even the more modern Hackneys which developed in the eighteenth century had the high action, the exaggerated lifting of the knees and hacks, which today is synonymous with the name; for such action reduces the ground that can be covered. Nevertheless, they were fine-looking, fast-moving animals.

After Arabian stallions were imported into England to breed with the native stock, there was an intense interest in the improvement not only of the Gallopers (the English Thoroughbreds with which we usually associate these Arabian stallions), but also of both Trotting Horses and Amblers. In breeding these imported stallions to native mares it was soon found that, whereas the progeny from many mares took to the gallop and so became valuable as racers, in others the predisposition to trot or, as the case might be, to amble, was so strong that the progeny, generation after generation, retained this predisposition. It was through crossing the Arabian with the mares who trotted and who passed on their predisposition to trot that the Hackney as well as the Standardbred (especially the Hambletonian) were developed.

One of the outstanding stallions of the eighteenth century was a horse called Blaze, who lived from 1733 to 1756. The preponderance of his blood was Arabian. His sire, a well-known Thoroughbred named Flying Childers, was sired by the Darley Arabian out of Betty Leeds, a mare with predominently Arabian, Turkish, and Barb bloodlines. Blaze's dam was the Conferate Filly. She had Turkish and Barb bloodlines also, but both her granddams were native mares of unknown breeding. Old records show that the modern English Hackney traces back to Blaze.

INTRODUCTION AND DEVELOPMENT OF THE HACKNEY IN THE NEW WORLD

The earliest official record of the introduction of English Hackneys goes back to the importation of a stallion named Bellfounder, foaled in 1816. Bellfounder's pedigree traces directly back to Blaze. Even before his importation, Bellfounder was outstanding, being thought the best Trotting Horse ever bred in England. A bright bay with black points, he stood fifteen hands in height. He had the typical sturdy build of the Hackney and the aristocratic small head and ears. For twenty years he lived in the United States and one of his most famous daughters was the Kent Mare, dam of Rysdyk's Hambletonian.

The importation of Bellfounder and his popularity as a sire was followed by the arrival of other outstanding English Hackneys. A large consignment went to Canada in 1881, and among them was the stallion Forham, son of Denmark who was the famous Foundation Sire of the American Saddle Horse. These horses were the property of the Honorable M. H. Cochrane of Quebec, and their progeny quickly spread through all of Canada and down into the United States.

As the years went on, more and more English Hackneys were imported, the breed became popular not only as Road Horses but also in the show rings.

CHARACTERISTICS

One of the Hackney's characteristics which sometimes is not associated with the breed is his ability to jump. The courageous spirit and the strong muscles which make him a great horse have also given him a tremendous spring. This was especially brought out in the show rings of twenty years ago when the famous Hackney stallion Sir Gilbert and his progeny began winning consistently in Open Jumper classes.

Sir Gilbert had been a show stallion in Hackney classes when he became blinded in one eye. He was retired to stud but insisted on jumping out of his paddock. The fence was raised and raised again until it was over five feet in height, but Sir Gilbert continued to sail over it. His owner, who decided that he was missing a bet, brought him back to the show ring as an Open Jumper and showed him successfully in all the top shows. Not only that, but his progeny inherited his ability. I remember seeing the horse at the age of eighteen in an exciting jump-off against his own four-year-old son.

Hackney Ponies, much more common today in the United States than Hackney Horses, were discussed in the Pony Division.

The American Hackney Horse Society was incorporated in 1891. Its purpose was to improve the breed and promote the breeding of Hackney horses and ponies as well as to publish, annually, a stud book of these animals. This society continues to be active. Although the original purpose of the Hackney as a road animal disappeared with the advent of automobiles, the increased interest in showing, especially of Hackney Ponies, has kept the breed alive.

The Morgan Horse

ORIGIN

Rightfully speaking, perhaps the Morgan should have been included in the Standardbred Division on the grounds that primarily he was a harness and general utility animal, one whose blood contributed largely to the development of the Standardbreds of today. But one might as well contend that he should be in the Saddlebred Division, for we find the pedigrees of both the Three- and Five-gaited Saddlers as well as the Tennessee Walkers tracing back to this sturdy, muscular, pony-sized phenomenon. The same thing occurs in our study of the Quarterhorse and other Western Stock horses, both the working ranch horses and the show horses. Taking this into consideration, the descendants of Justin Morgan should have a division all their own.

At West Springfield, Massachusetts, in the year 1747, a boy baby was born named Justin Morgan. His name was destined to live down through the ages, not for anything outstanding that he did himself (he was a singing teacher), but because in 1791 he accepted a two-year-old stallion in payment for a debt. Although the singing teacher had a farm in Springfield, he chose to bring his horse down to Randolph, Vermont. The colt was completely unbroken but so gentle that he amiably followed the singing master as the man

The inscription on the statue base reads:

1921
GIVEN BY
THE MORGAN HORSE CLUB
TO THE
U·S·DEPARTMENT OF AGRICULTURE
IN MEMORY OF
JUSTIN MORGAN
WHO DIED IN
1821

A statue of Justin Morgan *at the University of Vermont*

rode down the country lanes and through the logging trails. The colt was not a very prepossessing-looking animal, being small and short-legged. It was not his conformation but his amiability and his surprisingly well-developed muscles that appealed to the singing master.

He proved easy to train and became the singing master's favorite riding animal. In those days music teachers did a great deal of traveling, going from one local school to another, and Justin Morgan traveled on his colt all over upper New England and into Canada. No one even knows what name the colt was known by at this time nor if there was any particular record kept of his exact breeding. As far as can be ascertained, his sire is supposed to have been the war charger of General de Lancey. This was an imported Throughbred with two names: Beautiful Bay and True Briton. His dam may have been a mare of the Wild-air strain and thus part Thoroughbred. The Morgan Horse Club believes that the colt must have had a great deal of Arabian blood and possibly some Dutch.

The singing teacher, who was consumptive, lived only three more years, long enough to know that he had a very remarkable horse. The colt is supposed to have been able to outpull anything else on four legs in log dragging contests, to outtrot anything in harness and even to be a good jumper. Morgan considered gelding his horse at one point but decided first to put him to a few mares. Had the singing master's original intention been executed, the world would have never known the breed that carries his name, and perhaps our Standardbreds as well as our Saddlebreds and Quarterhorses would not have reached the point that they have today. But Justin Morgan, the man, died too soon to know that his stubby little stallion, due to his outstanding prepotency, was destined to be the only stallion ever to give his name to a distinctive breed of horse.

After his owner died in 1795, the young stallion, now a five-year-old, became the property of John Morgan, a relative, who called the colt after his original master. And now his fame began to spread. Lent for a year to a Robert Evans—a kind master but rather a poor provider—the little horse (he was only fourteen-one in height, a veritable pony) worked hard for his living. After hauling logs all day in the forests, he often showed his remarkable stamina and strength in contests in the evening. His get were also beginning to earn reputations, the most remarkable being their outstanding resemblance both physically and temperamentally to their sire. It is not surprising to find that, on Mr. Morgan's death, William Rice, of Woodstock, bid on the young stallion at once and bought him. He used him on his farm for two years, but Evans, who knew only too well what the horse could do, saved up his money and bought him back.

Again, Justin Morgan went back to the heavy labor in the woods. Unfortunately, Evans could not seem to get his financial affairs straightened out, and four years later, when he was sued for a debt, the horse was turned over to a Colonel John Goss, who sold him to his brother, David Goss, for a hundred dollars. The horse did ordinary farm work all year except for the two spring months when he was kept at stud. Philip Goss, David's son, was his next owner. Justin Morgan was now nineteen years old and he could not be expected to live forever. Lest he die on their hands, the Gosses turned him over to his old owner Evans for a year. It was while he was with Evans for the third time that Justin Morgan sired the famous Bulrush.

A year later, a Jacob Sanderson bought the horse and immediately sold him to a man named Langmade. Now in his twenties, the valiant little stallion for the first time began to show his age. Langmade worked him hard in a six-horse team and did not take particularly good care of him. He lost condition and was finally bought by a Mr. Chelsea, who sold him to another Goss (Joel), of Claremont, New Hampshire. At the end of the year he again changed hands, having been sold to Samuel Stone, and so found himself back in his original home, Randolph, Vermont.

Three years later the old stallion was sold to Levi Bean, who took him to his farm in Chelsea, Vermont. He was still sound in wind and limb, still able to do a day's work and still able as a sire. With his tremendous stamina he might well have lived to set a record for longevity but, unfortunately, at the age of twenty-nine he was kicked. The wound was neglected and the brave little stallion died.

One hundred years after his death, in 1921, the Morgan Horse Club gave a statue of Justin Morgan to the United States Department of Agriculture. This statue shows a horse with an enormous chest, neck and shoulder, a long barrel, rather small haunches, short legs, proudly carried head and a true "look of eagles." Not all of the Morgans seen today resemble their ancestor in conformation, but the Morgan head and neck are not to be mistaken. The Morgan disposition is also well known. It is said that the only thing Justin Morgan really disliked was a small dog and that he would not tolerate one in his paddock but chase it out immediately. From experience I can say that every Morgan we have ever owned has also disliked dogs.

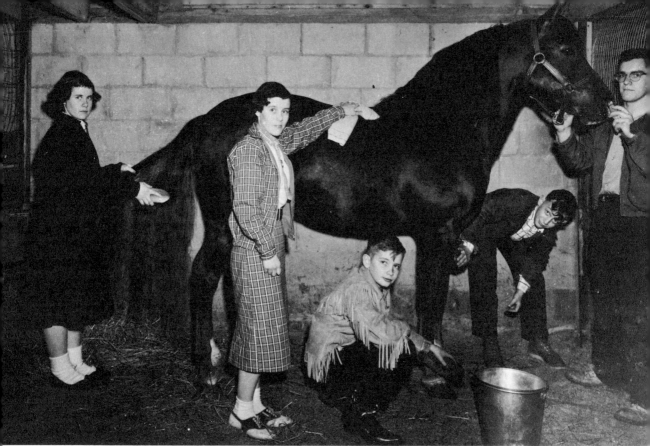

Frank Forword

Easter Twilight, *a Morgan stallion of today*

DEVELOPMENT

Justin Morgan founded three great families of Morgans. The Bulrushes, mostly browns and bays with no white markings at all, were noted in Vermont. The Woodburys, also from Vermont, were finer looking and sometimes had white markings on their heads. From the Sherman family came the well-known Black Hawk family mentioned before in the section on Standardbreds. Ethan Allan, one of the world's most famous harness horses, was of the Black Hawk family.

There are three distinct types of Morgans being bred today, the Show Morgan, the Stockhorse, and the Trail Horse. Of the three, the latter probably resembles most their distinguished ancestor both in appearance and disposition. Only a few years ago in Vermont I saw a two-year-old Morgan stallion that might almost have posed for the statue of old Justin. Furthermore, these "pleasure" horses are being bred as general utility animals under the saddle and in harness. They have proved particularly outstanding in long trail-ride competitions such as the Vermont Hundred Mile Ride, which takes place each fall at Woodstock, Vermont. They make ideal horses for boys and girls and are one of the most popular breeds in the 4-H Club programs. Several of the state agricultural colleges have Morgan Horse programs, using this breed to interest their students in the care and breeding of horses.

The Saddle-type Morgan of today is diverging more and more from the original type. Shoeing, training, selective breeding, etc., have produced a horse that is a good-looking, flashy animal but hardly portrays what we picture as a Morgan. Nevertheless, they have their place in the shows, and breeders and owners are doing much to increase the interest in the breed for this purpose.

Purebred Morgans are still found on the ranch as well as in the shows and rodeos out West. Here their agility, speed, and stamina have made them very valuable as Reining and Cutting Horses. Purebred Morgan Stallions are often bred with Quarterhorse mares to produce Stock Horses.

The Morgan Horse Club's headquarters is in West Hartford, Connecticut, at the following address: P.O. Box 2157, Bishop's Corner Branch. This is an extremely active club with an excellent monthly official publication called *The Morgan Horse Magazine*. The registry is now "closed," meaning that only animals with registered sires and dams are accepted for the list. They must be registered before they are three years old. Animals with "wall" or "watch" eyes (eyes without dark pigmentation in the iris) or with white markings above the knee or hock, except on the face, are not eligible. Registration papers must be submitted by the owner of the dam and signed also by the owner of the sire. The number of registrations is growing each year and will probably continue to increase due to the enormous growth of interest in every kind of competition for which the Morgans are eligible.

Just Plain Horse

All the major breeds of horses and ponies which are popular today in the United States have now been discussed. But we have not touched on that unsung hero of which there is a tremendous number, the horse (and especially the pony) of no particular known ancestry. This is the animal most often offered for sale at the dealers or on the auction block. To be sure, in almost every case there is a story of royal blood somewhere along the line, but it is never in writing. The buyer must, by scrutiny and his own experience, determine whether or not this is a suitable animal for his purpose, and it is usually several weeks before he actually knows what he has bought.

Yet it is this type of animal which most often finds its way into the stable of the private owner. The amateur wants a horse or pony because he loves them. He wants an animal that will be in its truest sense a pleasure horse. In this way the unregistered horse who must stand alone on his own merits and cannot expect to be kept and coddled because of his bloodlines retains a place which was common in the days before the machine age. He is a member of the family. Usually his owner is a teen-ager, generally a girl. The location of his home is often in a rural district. If there is a pony club or 4-H Club in the neighborhood, he will compete with other animals of his class for recognition. Especially in the South and West, he and others like him will find a place where, in riding, training, and in local competition his young owner will learn much more than the horse.

Even in the big Recognized shows these horses sometimes make names for themselves. Their most outstanding opportunity is in the Open Jumper classes. Here performance alone counts, and many a horse, including the famous Snowman, have risen from plebeian backgrounds to take top honors. In Western Performance classes, in Equitation classes both under English and Western Tack, and in children's Pet and Hunter Pony classes, the horse or pony that performs the best will find himself on the top of the judge's card.

His other great role today is as the school horse in camps, schools, hunt clubs, and riding academies. Here his life may be a hard one, for in the United States there is as yet no license required for the opening of a riding academy; no inspections are made, and the conditions in many are unspeakable. But in the stables run by real horsemen this is not so. The animals are well cared for, never overworked, and thoroughly appreciated. Undoubtedly, 90 per cent of today's young horsemen are riding, or learned to ride, on horses or ponies which have never been registered in any stud book and whose ancestry would be hard to trace.

There is probably a hint of royal blood in most horses: the high-held tail or the special gait of the Saddler, the beautiful throttle and delicate head of the Arabian, the typical crest of the Morgan, the long, lean lines of the Thoroughbred, the bunchy muscles of the Quarterhorse, or the compactness of the Hackney, are all indicative. Before buying an animal on these terms, be sure that the dealer has spotted the same characteristics and has a story prepared to back up his and your opinion. But the fact remains that there are outstanding horses who may bear resemblance not to one but to several breeds and whose true ancestry is buried in the past.

I should like to mention two of these that it has been my good fortune to own. The first was a thirteen-hand pony whom we called Sweetheart, and very well named she was. I could not possibly guess what breeds went into the making of this pony. She was built more like a small horse than a pony, and somewhat resembled the Standardbred in the height of her quarters, the Thoroughbred in the head and neck. She was a dark, almost liver chestnut, and we bought her from a local dealer after a ten-minute trial in a miserable paddock.

At that time my riding school was young and so were its clients. I needed ponies suitable for beginners ranging in age from five to ten years. The mounts had to have easy gaits, be completely reliable in disposition, and be willing to go out on the roads and trails, while staying automatically in line, one behind the other, under the disturbing and ignorant hands of the young beginner. Sweetheart, besides being pretty, which was the least of my requirements, so fully lived up to my specifications that her name would probably head any list of perfect children's mounts.

She was not only docile, but actually undertook responsibility above and beyond the call of duty. I remember returning home once at the head of a line of beginners. We were within sight of the stable, riding on the edge of a public road along which vehicles of every description passed at unknown intervals. In some ways this is more dangerous than riding beside a constantly traveled highway; for in the latter case both the children and the animals, realizing the danger, keep automatically to the side. But on Carter Street, where, during wartime there was not much traffic, vague children quite often allowed their ponies to wander out into the middle of the road. Looking back over my shoulder, I noticed that this had happened. Sweetheart, being assigned as usual to the least-talented of the group, was exactly in the middle of the road.

"Jimmy," I called to the inattentive six-year-old who was supposedly in command," Jimmy, get back into line, pull hard on your right rein and use your legs; you're right out in the road, and a car might come along." Obediently Jimmy tried. He pulled as hard as he could on his *left* rein (what six-year-old knows one from the other in times of stress?), bending poor

Sweetheart's head completely away from the direction in which I wanted her to go. But the little mare understood even if the child did not, and she obediently stepped back into line against the direct pull of the opposite rein.

When we reached the stable we had another problem. It was the rule for the line to pass between the stable door and the ring, continue on and turn left into the indoor hall, where they could be dismounted in safety. Each child gave the correct aides for the turn until it came to Jimmy. The child pulled with his right rein as hard as he could, turning the mare's head toward the enticing stable door beyond which lay her supper. But Sweetheart knew her duty; bracing her head against the rein, she obediently turned left and followed on into the hall, where she stopped and faced the center without any further hindrance from her rider.

It was only a short time after we bought Sweetheart that we found she was an outstanding jumper, and from then on she won many ribbons in both the Pony Jumper and Hunter classes. Here again she showed a willingness and intelligence that was phenomenal. But I should like to tell one more story to show what I consider Sweetheart's outstanding characteristic—her sense of responsibility.

She had been in the stable several years, but no one had ever tried her out in a cart. One autumn we got a new, light, two-wheeled vehicle to be used as a breaking cart in training the yearlings. One evening the children asked if Sweetheart "knew how to drive." "I don't know," I said: "I'll try her out tomorrow." So the next day while the children were at school I fitted her to some harness and took her into the indoor ring where I started all the young stock. I quickly realized that this was a new game to the little mare. She looked startled when she sensed the cart following at her heels. She did not understand the pressure of the shafts when I turned her, but, as always, she was willing to learn, and at the end of half an hour she was trotting around the ring with no signs of fear, though still a little uncertain as to what was expected of her.

"How did Sweet go?" asked the children at supper.

"She went quietly, though she doesn't know too much," I told them.

The next day I went to New York on business and arrived home at dusk. As usual the station yard held a mass of commuters' cars, snaking their ways around each other in an effort to be the first to leave. To my horror I caught sight of a pony cart. It was Gincy, aged seven and a half, and by no means an expert "whip." She was driving Sweetheart. Sitting beside her was the six-year-old child of a neighbor, a neighbor who was rather particular about what her children were allowed to do. I learned later that Gincy's older brother, home from school, had suggested the trip. As the young driver swung the little mare into the melee of vehicles, I saw that they were followed by our two bloodhounds who added their great voices to the general confusion.

I could do nothing except take my car from where it was parked and try to catch up with them. When I finally did, they were out of the village, safely bowling along the highway on the way home. Sweetheart, even though it was her first time in public between shafts, and even though she must have found the trains and the traffic terrifying, took charge and brought the adventure to a successful conclusion!

The second such equine character which we owned was Sky Rocket. One day I came home from a ride to find one of the most miserable specimens of horseflesh I have ever seen tied at one end of the ring. About fourteen hands and two inches, a bay, he perfectly fitted the description "crowbait." He was nothing but a skeleton with tightly stretched skin over it; and bare patches, open sores, cuts, and bruises covered him. As I approached he shrank back. Yet, in spite of his ugliness, somehow there was the famed "look of eagles" in his eyes. He was bloody, literally, but he was unbowed.

There was another horse tied up at the other end of the ring, a common enough Western "chunk" type. I was told that one of the dealers, thinking I might need a good school horse, had dropped the latter off for me to look at while he went somewhere else. The little bay had had to be unloaded, for he was the animal nearest the tailgate. On his way back the dealer was planning to leave the bay with the "knacker" to be destroyed and turned into dogmeat.

The chunk turned out to be clumsy, bad-tempered, and thoroughly unsuitable. I turned my attention again to the little bay. After a moment he let me approach him and only quivered lightly as I stroked his neck. He was almost the exact size and color of Meadow Whisk, our little Thoroughbred stallion described earlier. It had been only the day before that the veterinary had told me that Whiskey's useful days were numbered because of the ophthalmia. Certainly this pathetic excuse for a horse was a far cry from our lovely Whisky, but still, there was that look of eagles....

I got a snaffle pony bridle to fit the delicate head and a light saddle. I could not look at his teeth to judge the age for he was far too head shy, but he looked like a mature though quite young animal. (Later I was to learn that he was only four years old.) After a few minutes he let me put on the tack. When I mounted, his back sank under my weight, for he was obviously weak from starvation. My idea was just to walk and jog trot him to see if he had any really bad habits, if he were sound, and what his gaits were like.

The instant he moved out I realized that this was no common horse, for he strode with a delicate, light step and the forward impulsion of the highly bred, hot-blooded horse. He was extremely flexible, and his mouth, though not too highly educated, was unspoiled.

"Put a six-inch bar up; I'll just trot him across it," I said. So jumping standards and a low bar were set up. I turned the little horse toward the obstacle. His ears came forward, he gathered himself and, with no signal from me, started for it at the canter. I left my reins loose, not knowing what to expect. If he were a trained jumper, which I did not believe he was, all would be well. If he were unschooled, anything might happen. Before a horse learns to jump properly he has to learn to determine the exact height of the obstacle. When his head is raised, his eyes show him only a fuzzy outline, and this, after much practice, he gradually learns to interpret. Until then he is apt to stop, shy out of fear, or overjump because he does not know the real height and is afraid of hitting it. In such a case even the experienced horseman may make a mistake and punish the mouth of his mount.

When we reached the low bar, the little horse did not hesitate but sprang into the air. And what a spring! In our indoor hall the window sills are five feet from the ground level. The several onlookers all assured me that at the height of the jump the little horse's feet were well above the height of the sills!

Then he returned to earth, and to disaster, for in his weakened condition he could not possibly hope to support the combination of my weight and his under the force of the landing. Down on his nose he went. I found myself straddling him, both feet on the ground. But he was so agile and full of courage that he scrambled up again under me.

Such heart was rare. The dealer, who had returned, was standing in the doorway. In five minutes the deal was concluded, and Sky Rocket (there was only one possible name for him after seeing the way he had soared through the air) was mine for fifty dollars. Had the dealer not come in in time to see that jump, I could have had him for the price of his carcass—ten dollars. But I did not begrudge it.

We spent the next six months getting some flesh on his bones and heal-

Sky Rocket *jumps through a balloon hoop.*

ing the cuts. Then we started training him as a jumper. Sky Rocket, like Whiskey, was a natural. He was timid, nervous, terribly headshy, and took a rider with sensitive hands, but no one had either to teach him how to jump or to instill the love of jumping in him. He had been born with both the knowledge and the love.

We tried putting him out in a paddock one day to enjoy the fresh green grass. Rocket was not interested in grass. He leaped the four-foot, six-inch panel fence, galloped down the pasture, hopped over the single strand three-foot electric wire fence into the road, returned along the road, jumped back into the paddock, out again and repeated the circle. It took us nearly an hour to coax him away from his idea of fun on a Sunday afternoon. After that we never turned him out alone except into the indoor hall. In company and in the big fields he was more content to "stay put."

One winter we had a tremendous blizzard. Rocket loved snow and so we let him, Lark, and a few of the others out into the big pasture for a run. The others went off together but Rocket discovered a snow-covered stone wall separating two fields. The bank of snow must have been nearly five feet in height and well over ten feet in width, but Rocket spent all afternoon jumping back and forth over it just to feel the pleasure of soaring through the air!

No kind of jump fazed him. His specialty was mental-hazard jumping, and for years he was our star performer of this role in the circus. Yet in every other way he was excessively timid. I was sitting on him one day in the outdoor ring talking to some children, when a spectator a few steps away scratched a match. Before I could gather up my reins Rocket had cleared the double four-foot fence that surrounds the ring.

He became known throughout the locality for his jumping, as he invariably won. Twice he won the blue at Madison Square Garden against the best competition there was. Many a time has it been said to me that if he had been a hand higher, he would surely have ended up on the Olympic team.

Rocket had none of the physical characteristics one expects to find in an Open Jumper that must stay sound. His legs were delicate, he had very little bone, neither his chest nor his quarters were particularly well developed, and he had a short barrel though his ribs were not especially well sprung. In the stall, or standing, he looked like nothing; but in the jumping ring he changed and took on the beauty of flight. He always had to jump fast, and he liked contact throughout the approach, flight, and landing; but he made his own decisions as to take off and rate, and he *never* made a mistake. Sky Rocket had the greatest heart of any of our horses and ponies. He lived to be almost twenty, and the day when he had to be put down, because of respiratory ailments, is one I would not like to live through again.

These are the horses of today. It will be interesting to see just how the picture develops. Will only the horses that can qualify as "moneymakers" survive; the race horses and show horses whose value is rated in five or more figures? Will there be only professional horsemen left—the jockeys, trainers, and show riders? Or will the inherent love of horses and the psychological uplift that comes to a person who finds himself atop a horse be enough to insure the continuance of the amateur who rides for the love of it and of the horse wanted for that purpose?

Only time can tell.